Foreword

Two school friends from the same foreign land, almost the same age, arrived to the same country, in the same year, on the same ship, lived in the same suburb and went to the same schools met up again after a long, almost 40 year gap.

Why one of us, now grown men, would decide to meet up is an unknown mystery of life, like many other journeys in our lives, paths we take, some that are created for us and some that are destined for us to follow and how, one day I was destined to meet Vito Radice, *"The Don"*.

One day, I found out about this Political Party called *"The Humanist Party"*, and the name *"Vito Radice"*.

Hey, I said, that's *"Vito Radice from my high school days at Drummoyne Boys'"*.

This never left my mind and for many, many, years I remembered my friend Vito had formed a Political Party here in Sydney, Australia.

We finally met with the help of Facebook, at a little cafe in Haberfield where we sat and reminisced about our childhood years at Drummoyne Boys', the chicks, the teachers, the students etc.

Vito Radice, I recall, had a creative streak out of the norm and challenging the of opinions with some teachers as I observed in some instances. Yes, *"The Don"* was in the "smarter" classes with the elite, the ones that learnt quickly and easily which led Vito to Uni. I considered Vito a smart kid on par with the elite kids but also being modest and cooperative with everybody.

In art classes, Vito once painted a picture which captured my imagination and the teacher's as well. I remember them gazing at the painting and quietly making comment The painting, was a group of hands large and small with pointy fingers in a myriad of colours and in detail *(almost psychedelic looking)* which made you stare into it trying to look for something else within the painting.

It was in the final two years of High School that our lives took a different direction. *"The Don"*, went on to Uni and I went overseas and we never met up again.

Today, Vito Radice, *"The Don"*, has written and published many short stories a talent I never knew he had, about his life, the era, the music and his adventures, including his poems with a "twist".

His books, in particular *"My Life with Chickens and Other Stories"*, truly tell it as it was and his frank and openness about everything in his life and the people in his journey through life is to be admired for its honesty and truthfulness.

"Poems for Misfits, Miscreants, Misanthropes, Mavericks, Losers and Malcontents", a masterpiece of personal thoughts on, any subject, time and event, all scrambled into poetic verse with logical meaning.

What about, *"Poems for Restless Minds & Restless Hearts"*, what a title. Don't we all go through this stage at least once in our life time. Here you will find poems on anything that will surely put you at ease. *"The Don's"*, view and "spin" on things that will get you deep in thought with a little "chuckle" at the same time.

Followed by, *"Poems for Troubled Minds & troubled souls"*. A book on *"The Don"* himself, versed in poems that don't have to rhyme and don't stick to the same pattern, but do describe the author's inner thoughts with no inhibitions.

Another of *"The Don's"* most fascinating book is, *"My Life in a Cult & other stories"*. It's not the "CULT" we are all led to believe but, an autobiography on *"The Don's"* political career, his adventures, people in his life, the contributions, his mentors some famous quotes that brought meaning to life and hot topics of the times back in Australian Politics and world events.

You will be pleased to see the myriad of "classic songs" and writings from famous musicians *"The Don"* uses as backdrops in some pages of most of his books, just to stir up that emotion and bring the reader closer to the subject matter and era.

Having met Vito Radice again, after almost 40 years with only memories of earlier school years, with pleasure and surety I say he is a compassionate person, a remarkable sense of humour, intelligent, an extremely good listener and definitely non-judgmental and friendly.

I say, his book titles are "bizarre", his poems can be "bizarre", his choice of vocabulary "not mainstream" but then, in a world of perfection and Artificial Intelligence his stories and "style" is HUMANISTIC.

I am grateful for having a good friend like Vito Radice *"The DON"*.

You friend,
Jack Sciara
October, 2020

Who was to know, that two wogs from the same foreign land, almost the same age should arrive at the same city in the same country in the same year on the same ship, live in the same suburb and go to the same schools and then, loose contact after "6th form" and reconnect via Facebook 40 years later.

"The Don", Vito and I grew up in the Inner west and stayed there.
Our parents must have felt comfortable being around other Italians and close to their places of employment.

In 1965, the Inner west was an even mixture of Anglo and European Nationals. The schools, the factories, the shops all one big "melting pot" of cultures, all trying to make a living, assimilate and be accepted as "equals" and not guests.

"MY LIFE AS A WOG: WOG BOY- I AM A WOG & I'M PROUD" is to me, a sequel to *"The Don's"* 2019 edition of *"My life with Chickens and other stories"* and, in order to fully appreciate this edition, you must read this in depth look at the "growing up" life of the author and the Radice Family.

"The Don", has written many books and, if you are new to his style, don't be shocked by his sincerity and sense of humour.

Having read almost all his books, I came to realise, Vito has a unique style of language which reflects an individual identity, the type of man, his experiences, his wisdom.

Though, his poems may not be mainstream poetry, the reader must not confuse the context for the "true character" of this writer, as this is prevalent in the Forwards written by those that know him well.

I write these few words as an introduction to a plethora of Vito's quirky readings in his poetry and of course, a down to earth reflection (in this book) of *"how life was for a wog boy in the 60's"*.

Happy reading.
:):)
Jack Sciara
September, 2022

Jack Sciara

"This book is dedicated to my father, Giuseppe Radice and my mother, Angela Martone without whom I would not exist!"

-Vito Radice ("The Don")
10th September 2021

Birthplace (Origins)
(Luogo di Nascita (Origini))

He was born in a small village.
High on the side of a mountain.
Called *"San Fele"*.
In the southern region of *"Basilicata"*, Italy.
Its capital is called *"Potenza"*.
It means *"Strength"* in English.
And maybe there is some truth in this.
The people from this region are a proud & resilient bunch.
Authentic.
They've experienced the pitfalls, hardships & tribulations that life throws at you.
You can see it etched on their faces.
But they are survivors.
They are as tough as steel & then some.
But they are also humble folk.
No time for pretentiousness here.
Whatever they have, which is not much...
...they'll gladly share it with *"paesane"*.
If you happen to walk by.

They worked the land.
That unforgiving earth.
Removing stones with their bare hands.
And carrying them away on their backs.
They still ploughed the land with a cow drawn plough in 1964.
Life was tough.
As touch as it comes.
Some might even call it *"brutal"*.
But they had no other way to live...
...to survive.
This was their life.
This had been their life.

Until one day his whole world was about to change...
...forever.
With his mother & older brother, they immigrated to Sydney, Australia.
"The land of milk & honey".
"The promised land."
There he was reunited with his father that he had never seen before.
Life was tough for him.

But this was not new.
He had always had a tough life.
He knew what he had to do...
...to survive & prosper in this unforsaken backwater.

Then one day, in 1972.
A film was released called *"The Godfather"*.
A film considered by many to be one of the best films ever made.
High praise indeed.
The main character *"The Godfather"*, was called *"The Don"*...
...*"I'll Padrino"*.
...*"The Godfather"*
His name was *"Don Vito Corleone"!*

And so, his identity was chosen for him.
His friends soon started to call him *"Don"*.
He liked it.
It stuck.
"The Don" was born!

"The Don"
14.03 2022

Bloody WOGS!

(Maledetti WOGS!)

We're too loud.
We talk with our hands.
We don't respect rules.
We don't respect the law.
We write our own.
In fact, we have our own giver of punishment...
...the Mafia.
We are those...
...bloody WOGS!

We create chaos.
We're anarchic.
We're anarchists.
We do what the fuck we want.
We don't give a shit.
We have our own code.
We are those...
...bloody WOGS!

You can either join us or...
...be against us.
We don't need you, anyway!
It is you who need us.
We are the ones that make you.
We are the excitement.
We are the energy.
We are the *POWER*.
We are the *creative force*.
Yep...
...those...
...bloody WOGS!

(WOGS is a derogatory term for Southern European immigrants used in Australia during the 1960s & 1970s)

"The Don"
06.02.2022

I am a WOG: WOG Boy

I am not a native of this land.
I was not born here.
I was born in another place & time.
I was born in Southern Italy.
I am a WOG Boy.

I am an immigrant.
I had no choice in the matter.
I was not asked if I wanted to come here.
I was brought out with my mother & brother.
I am a WOG Boy.

I came out on a huge ocean liner.
It was called "The Galileo".
I'd never seen an ocean before.
I'd never seen a boat before.
I am a WOG Boy.

I was 5 years young.
I came from a farm in southern Italy.
We were poor.
There was very little food.
I am a WOG Boy.

I was a happy.
I played with my cousins.
I played with my faithful companion "Sargento".
He was my protector, my guardian, my friend, my dog.
I am a WOG Boy.

I had a happy childhood.
Until I was 5 years young.
Then I was brought to another country.
I was transplanted to "Terra Australis", Australia.
I am a WOG Boy.

It was December 1964.
When I set foot in another country.
This country known as the "Great Southern Land".
"The land of hope & opportunity".
I am a WOG Boy.

My life changed forever.
I was a curly, redheaded, freckled skinned boy from a foreign land.
I ate different food.
Spoke a different language.

I had a weird name...
"Vito".
"Radice".
WTF, sorta name is that?
Many times, I wanted to change my name.
(In fact, I did once. I called myself Victor.
Bad move. It didn't work out well. But I digress, that's another story).
Wore different clothes.
Sang different songs.
Had a different culture.
I was not from here.
I was not accepted.
I was panted.
I was taunted.
I was bullied
I was laughed at.
I was ridiculed.
I was humiliated.
I felt ashamed.
I cried.
I was alone.
I was sad.
I was not happy.
I did not fit in.
I did not want to be who I was.
I wanted to be an "Aussie"!
But...
...I was a WOG Boy.

I am a WOG!

"WOG" was a derogatory, racist word used to put down immigrants from southern Europe during the 40s, 50s, 60s & 70s in Australia under the "White Australia Policy".
It is now a "badge of honour"!

"I am a WOG & I am proud!"
"I'm a WOG BOY!"
"Shout it out LOUD!"
"I'm a WOG BOY!"
"& I am proud!"
"I'm a WOG BOY!"

"I am a WOG!"

"The Don"
21.05.2021
May, 2021

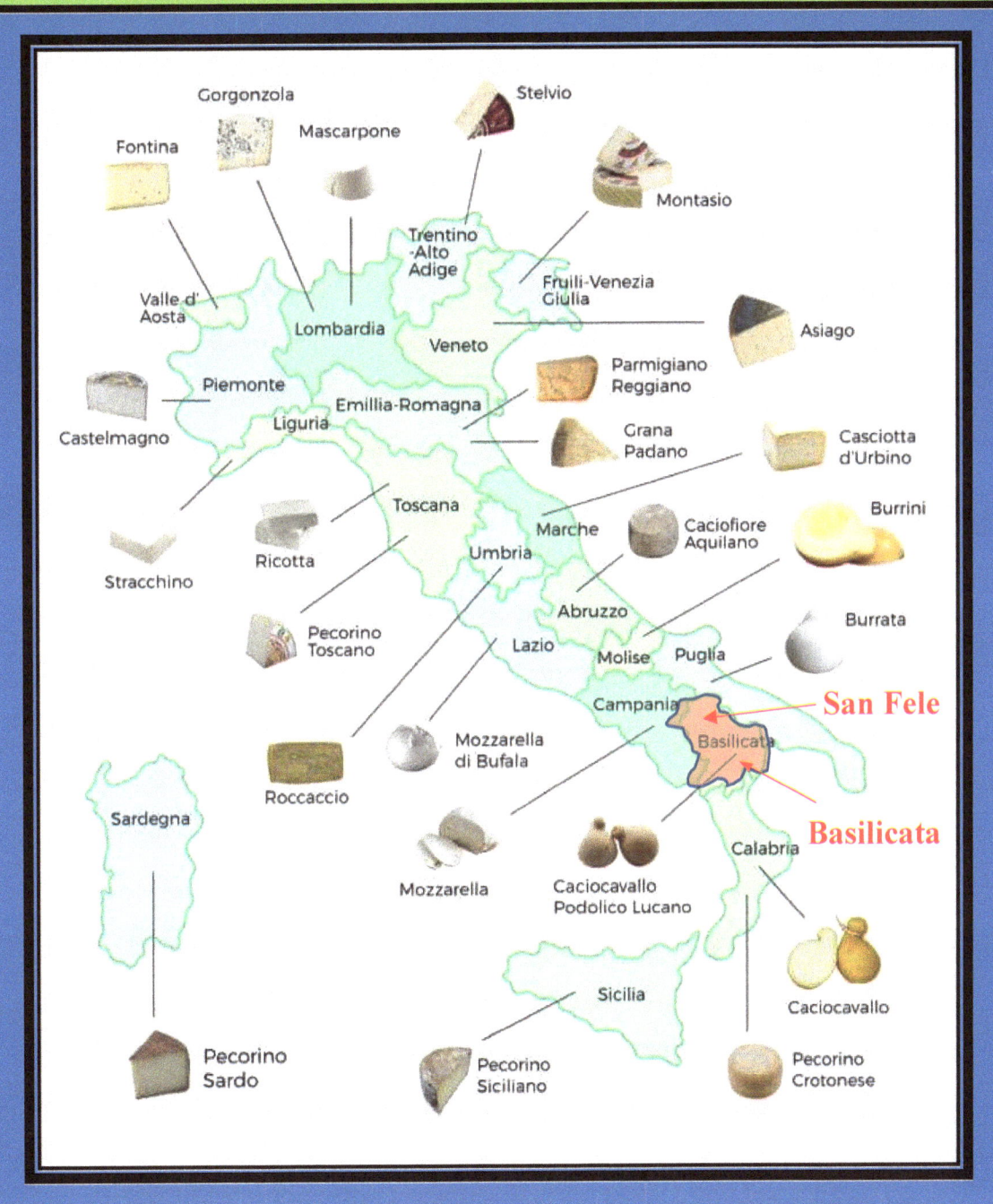

Contents:

Part 1: The Old World
(The days of innocence/The "Halcyon Days")

Chapter 1: My Father: Giuseppe Radice   13
Chapter 2: My Mother: Angela (Martone) Radice   19
Chapter 3: My Story Begins……The Farm: DIFESA   23
Chapter 4: The Sea Voyage   27

Part 2: The New World
(The "Lucky Country"/The land of "Milk and Honey")

Chapter 5: The New Land: The Journey Begins   29
Chapter 6: School Days   35
Chapter 7: My Life with Chickens!   42
Chapter 8: Sydney: A simpler Time!   46
Chapter 9: Death, God, Religion, Love and Masturbation   52
Chapter 10: Family Time! A Bonding Time!   54
Chapter 11: Other Yummy "Wog" Treats   65
Chapter 12: The Golden Chariot   71
Chapter 13: In Search of the Meaning in Life   74
Chapter 14: Living in the 1970s & 80s   80
Chapter 15: My Life in a CULT   88
Chapter 16: The Community for Human Development   90
Chapter 17: The (Great) Escape *(from the nest)*   102
    I gotta get outta of this place!
Chapter 18: "The Humanist Party"   105
Chapter 19: "The Radice Code"   119
Chapter 20: The Evolution of "The Don"   122
Chapter 21: "Buona Vita-Be Creative"   126
Chapter 22: In the End…   128

Part 1: The Old World
(The Days of Innocence/The "Halcyon Days")

Chapter 1: My Father: Giuseppe Radice

The old farmhouse with Pierno & Santa Croce in the background
Photo circa 1970

My father was a very simple man. He only wanted a simple and uncomplicated life.

He liked fresh air and sheep. He did not like people or the company of people much. *"Never trust the people"* was his mantra and he repeated this often (maybe, this is where I get my love of repeating words and phrases over and over again).

Giuseppe was born in a small Italian village called *San Fele* in the province of *Basilicata* on 10th September 1924. Until 1960 he lived a simple life as a subsistence farmer (with his father Nicola, the patriarch and Sozomeno, his brother), working the land, milking the cow, looking after the sheep and going off to the village (which was about six kilometres away) on his beloved donkey.

He was not much of a thinker or interested in learning. He in fact only had six months of schooling, preferring to run away and sleep under the *"Ponte Vecchio"*, where he was often found, rather than sit in a classroom. These were his halcyon days. His days of *"milk and honey"*. He would often reminisce about these days when he was not angry and throwing a tantrum. He could be "light" and cheerful, even funny and sometimes he even laughed, when he wanted to. But these times were very few a far between. For the man that I knew was a bitter and angry man, not the young boy sleeping under the *"Ponte Vecchio"*!

It was in 1960 that Giuseppe's whole world came tumbling down. Destroyed forever! He was told by his father that the farm could no longer sustain three families, someone had to leave and since he was the eldest, he had to go!
He cried! *"Why me?"* he screamed to my grandfather. *"Your brother has problems with his passport. It has to be you!"*. He ran away to the place that had been his sanctuary, under the *"Ponte Vecchio"*.

He was persuaded that life in "Australia" would be the best thing for him and his family, especially for his two young boys Nick and Vito. That this was NOT about his needs but to provide a BETTER future for them. Australia was the FUTURE! He cried even more! He cried because he knew he would NEVER come back! That this was FOREVER! A lifetime jail sentence for a crime he didn't know he had committed!

So, it came to pass that in 1960, Giuseppe left his beloved farm, *"Difesa"*, bordered the "Achilles Laura" ocean liner, the *"Marconi"* and came to Australia.

Bare in mind that Giuseppe had never seen the sea before. Let alone an enormous ship, on which he spent thirty-nine days for the journey to Australia.

1: Nonna Radice with her rabbits
2: Zio Sozomeno, Nonna, Nonno & Zia Rosa in front of the old farmhouse
Circa 1970

San Fele, Basilicata, Italia

San Fele

1: Brother, mother, me, 1961
2: Father, Nick (brother), mother, me, 1960
3: Father, 1959

1: Nonna Angela Radice and Nonno Nicolo Radice
2: Nonna Angela Radice and Nonno Nicolo Radice in Difesa
3: Nonno Nicola Radice in front of the old farmhouse
All photos circa 1960s
4: Zia Rosa Radice and Nonna Angela Radice in front of the old farmhouse
5: Nonna Angela Radice in front of the old farmhouse
6: Nonna Angela Radice in the vegetable garden

Chapter 2: My Mother: Angela (Martone) Radice

My mother was born on 5th May 1932. She married my father in 1950. She was just eighteen years old! My father was twenty-six years old.

Her family suffered through quite a few tragedies. Two of her brothers died early in their lives, Michael died when he was nine years old from appendicitis and Giuseppe died from a work place accident (he fell into a vat of molten metal) in Canada. He was twenty-six years old. Her youngest brother, Antonio had a nervous breakdown when he was eighteen years, from which he never fully recovered.

Her parents, Vito Martone (after whom I was named) and Angelamaria Martone (Carnevale) were the kindest people in the village. Everyone knew of them, respected and loved them. My grandfather, Nonno Vito, was nicknamed *(supranomo)*, *"Skertz"*, which loosely translated means "joker". Something which I seem to have inherited! He made everyone laugh and also made the best wine in the region.

My grandfather on my father's side, Nonno Nicolo, was nicknamed *(supranomo)*, *"Feffo"*, which loosely translated means "fool"!

People were referred to by the their *supranomo*, *"Nicolo U'Feffo"*, *"Vito Skertz"*.

These *supranomi* always seemed to refer to some derogatory aspects of that individual. The ones I remember were:

"Pisca Latte", Piss Milk,
"Sansa Sange", Without Blood,
"Morta Letto", Dead in Bed.

In those days, people didn't get married for love, they were arranged marriages. The parents of the boy would approach parents of the girl (usually the father) and ask if he was interested in marrying his daughter off to his son. The girl had no say in it! Land or money was usually involved in the discussions. It was a business transaction

At twenty-six years of age, my father was getting quite old and was not really interested in getting married. Nonno Nicola, had other ideas and knew that if he didn't marry Giuseppe off soon, it would become more difficult as he got older.

So, the deal was made!

Angela Martone married Giuseppe Radice and became Angela Radice.

My mother has often told me that when she married my father:

"I went from Heaven to Hell!"

My mother has since to told me that she asked her father, *"Why did you marry me off to him? His reply, "I didn't know! I'm sorry!"*

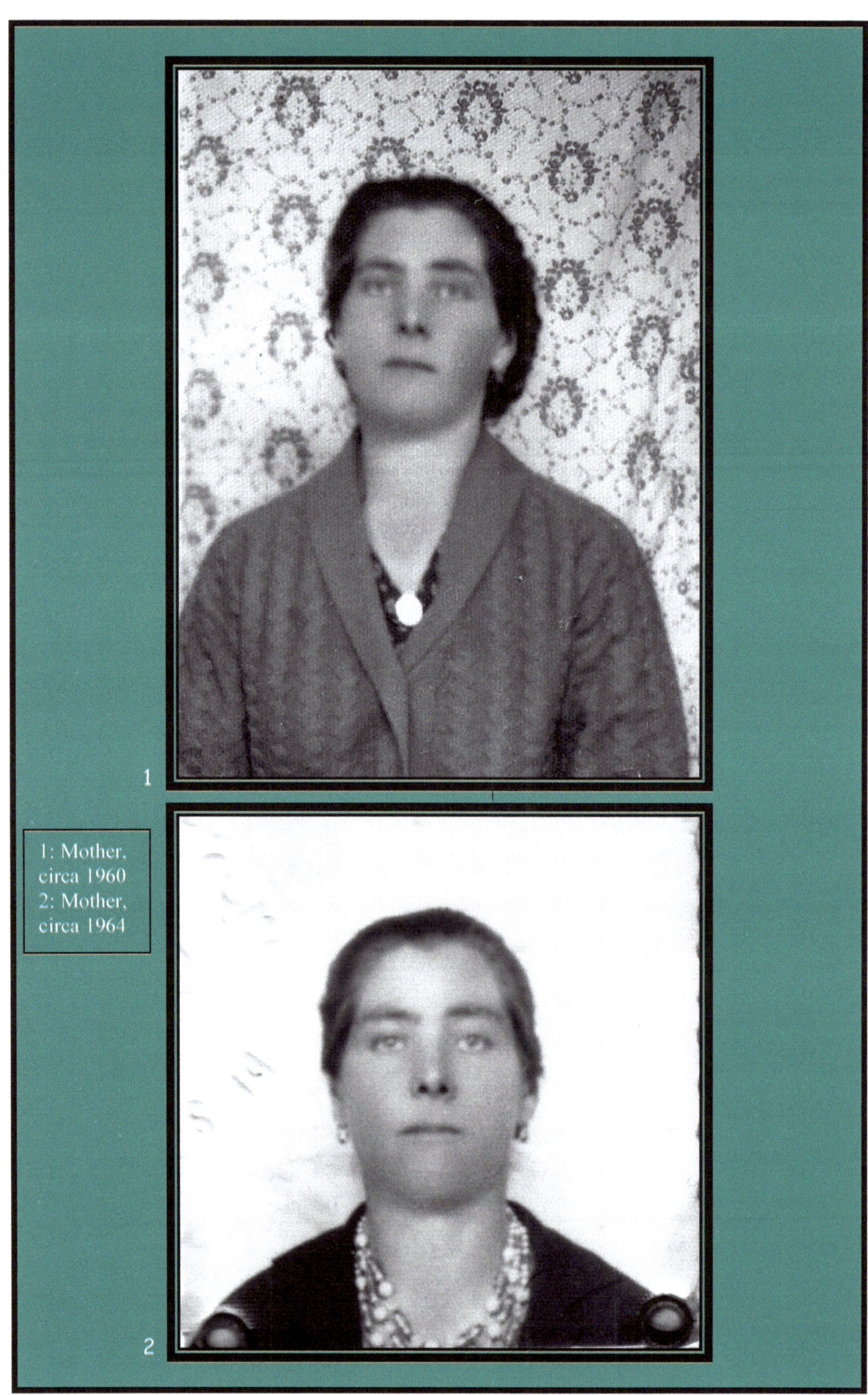

1: Mother, circa 1960
2: Mother, circa 1964

Mother and Father on their wedding day, she was 18 and he was 26 years old, 1950

1: Nonna Angelamaria Martone and Nonno Vito Martone
2: Zio Antonio Martone, Nonna Angelamaria Martone and Nonno Vito Martone
3: Mother and brother Nick at about two years old
4: Zio Giuseppe Martone died in an accident in Canada in 1959

Chapter 3:   My Story Begins……The Farm: DIFESA

The old farmhouse in Difesa, 1960. It was demolished in 1983

I was born on the 10th March 1959, in the Year of the Pig of the Chinese calendar, under the Astrological Sign of Pisces. I was born in the village of *San Fele*, in my Nonna Martone's house. The house is built into the side of the mountain and it's still there today. Abandoned!

My father wanted a boy and told her, "If it's not a boy, do not come back!". My mother tells me that she always wanted a girl and had hoped I would be a girl but God was not kind to her and instead she got me, another boy! This did not stop her though and apparently, she would dress me in girls' clothes as a baby. Apparently, I was very cute and adorable. Whom am I to argue?

The area of Basilicata that our farm was located in was called *"Difesa"*. According to a story my uncle Sozomeno told me, the reason why it was called this was that during the second world War, this area was the last line of defence or resistance against the Germans, *"Defence (English) Difesa"*.

There were two mountains directly to the right of the homestead, *"Pierno"* and *"Santa Croce"*.

We lived in a very simple three room building on a hill, my grandfather in the middle room, my uncle on the left side room and we had the right. We all lived in this one room. We cooked, ate and slept in this one room. Each contained a fireplace on which we cooked and the fire kept us warm. There was no internal water, which had to be fetched from a nearby well and no electricity. We used oil lamps to provide lighting at night which provided very little light and made the room quite dark and sooty.

Original "Off Grid Living"!

Electricity was being rolled into our region when we left in 1964, as we were leaving!

There were no toilets, showers or laundries of any sort. We had to do our ablutions behind the building. Washing ourselves and our clothes was done in the river, about a twenty-minute walk away.

One particular event that I remember vividly was when we had to have the baby calf in the room with us for almost a month. There were cow thieves targeting our region and under the cloak of darkness, they would go around to the different farms and whilst everyone was asleep, steal calves and lambs. So, to protect our valued calf, she lived with us. I actually liked it. She was very friendly and had kind eyes. Although, the smell of her poo was sometimes overbearing for my tender nostrils.

My grandfather was a hard task master and would make the family work on the farm from dawn till dusk seven days a week, summer and winter, every year. The summers were extremely hot and the winters were extremely cold. There were no machines to make the physical work any easier. Everything was done by hand, using very simple, ancient techniques, passed down through the generations. That's the way things were done, there was no point arguing or questioning it.

In spring and summer work was in ploughing, sowing, harvesting, staking and slaughtering. In the winter months it involved clearing the land which was not very fertile and full of rocks which had to be removed.

Everyone was involved in this work.

The land was worked with a wooden plough pulled along by a cow, just as in the Roman days. The wheat was sown by hand. The wheat was harvested by hand using a sickle and then bagged by hand. The hay was rolled by hand, moved by hand and stacked in the barn by hand.

Most of the wheat was sold off and the rest (the lower quality stuff, husks etc.) was left for our consumption. The wheat was ground by hand using two large stones to grind it down.

Cows and goat's milk was used to make cheese, which was predominantly sold with very little left for us. Pigs, lambs, chickens, rabbits, turkeys, pigeons, were slaughtered and the meat sold off. The off cuts and the offal were left for us to make salami, *"copa,"*, *"prosciutto"*, ham, pigs trotters and other cured meats.

No part of the slaughtered animal was thrown away. The blood was collected and eaten, the fat was used as lard for cooking, the offal was cooked and eaten.

Two delicacies of our region are *"Sfritt"*, a dish cooked after the slaughter of a pig. This was a big affair and involved at least eight men to hold it down. The pig was an enormous animal. It knew it was going to die a very horrible death. It did not want to die! After exsanguination, the draining of all of the pig's blood, it was collected and later cooked and eaten!

The festivities lasted all day and well into the night and most of the villagers came to celebrate and have a good time. *"Au'Sfrit"* was cooked around lunchtime and everyone claimed to have the BEST recipe. The basic ingredients common to all were: pig offal, pig blood, potatoes, onions, garlic and red capsicum in vinegar, all fried in a huge by pan, usually by a man, the owner of the pig. Of course, there were many variations of this.

The second delicacy was a *"blood cake"*. This was served in the evening with coffee as a dessert. The main ingredients were, fresh pig's blood, chocolate, sugar, milk cinnamon and other spices, all put into a cake pastry, with cross-work pastry strips on top and baked in the oven for about twenty minutes.

Both dishes were delicious!

Bread was made only once a month because it required a lot of wood to heat the stone oven. So once it was fired, enough bread was baked to last the whole month. Pizzas, frittatas *(an Italian omelette)*, sweets other foods were also cooked. Other nearby friends were also invited to use the fired-up oven to bake their bread as well. So *"baking day"* was also a day of festivity and celebration.

A story my mother loves to tell me was on one particularly hot summer day, when she was working the fields, she decided to send me back to the homestead with *"Sargente"* our dog. He was black and quite large and I must've been about 3 years old. My mother used to take me with her when she worked the fields because there was no one to look after me since everyone else was also out working the fields. She could see me walking with *Sargente* who would push me back in the right direction if I started to wander. She found me sleeping on *Sargente's* belly, who was also sleeping, underneath the cherry tree in front of the homestead.

Another time my mother gave me a piece of bread to eat, a little while later, she came back came and was surprised that I had already finished it so quickly. Apparently. *Sargente* had gently teased it out of my had with his teeth, ate it and then lay beside me sheepishly pretending to be innocent!

I loved *Sargente*. He was still alive when we left in 1964. I believe he lived a long life.

Me at 18 months, 1960

Chapter 4: The Sea Voyage

We spent a night in Naples with my grandparents *"Papanonno e Mamanonna d'paese, grandfather and grandmother from the village"*, (where we had to board the Ship. I had never left my village, let along seen a massive city like Naples or a huge ocean liner. I remember being very sad and crying because I didn't want to leave my grandparents (I was very close to them and I loved them a lot)!

On board we were placed in a four persons cabin with a solitary porthole window which we shared with another woman I'd never met before. It was very small and cramped but I had the top bunk so I was happier!

My brother and I were in complete awe at the size and grandeur of the ship. We had never seen anything like this. We used to get up really in the mornings and rush out for breakfast before anybody else was there. Laid out on an extremely long table, there were trays and trays heaped with food that we had never seen before! We used to just stand and stare at it trying to see if we could recognise anything. We did not!

The ocean was very rough at times and a lot of people got seasick. Fortunately, my brother and I did not and we would go off and explore the ship, when he felt kindly towards me. At other times he would go off on his own and I would be left with my mother. My brother is seven years older than me!

There were many stories from our journey but one particular one which sticks in my memory was the stormy night when a rumour spread through the ship that an inspection of all the cabins was going to take place. Apparently, people had smuggled on board cakes of cheese and jars of salami, assuming that these would not be available in Australia. So, in the middle of this dark, windy and stormy night with the ship rocking from side to side and water splashing onto the decks, rows of drenched women, dressed in black, clinging for their lives, tossed it all overboard.

There was no inspection!

We went through the Suez Canal and the trip lasted thirty-three days.

I was almost six years old when I arrived in Sydney on the 24th December 1964. I came with my mother and brother from a small village (called *"San Fele"*) in Italy where I was born.

We came over on an ocean liner called the *"Galileo"* and that's when I met my father for the very first time. He had been here since 1960. I remember this day vividly, as if it were just yesterday. The ship docked at *Circular Quay* and I was trying to see my father, but of course I had no idea what he looked like, but somehow, I still thought I would be able to recognise him from the many faces standing and cheering on the wharf.

Finally, we disembarked and somehow amongst the throng I was introduced to my father. I shook his hand, (our family never openly demonstrated love and affection with each other)!

My uncle was also there. He drove us to our new home *(Elizabeth Street, Five Dock)* in his brand new *1964 Chrysler Valiant Triptronic* with wings.

It was Christmas Eve!

The Galileo Ocean Liner
SS Galileo Galilei was an ocean liner built in 1963
She was scuttled in the Strait of Malacca in 1999

Part 2: The New World
(The "Lucky Country"/The Land of "Milk and Honey")
Chapter 5: The New Land: The Journey Begins

On his arrival to *"The New Land"*, he lived with my uncle (his brother-in-law), Zio Michaele Carnevale and his sister, my aunty, Zia Laura

My uncle was one of the very first to immigrate out to Australia, coming here in 1952, where he settled in Five Dock (an inner west suburb of Sydney). He had a vision and passion to get his *"paesane, (person or persons from the same village that are not directly related)*, out of the squalor and poverty of *San Fele*.

At the time, the Australian Government required a *"Sponser"* for someone to immigrate. The *"Sponser"* needed to provide two requirements for approval: shelter and a job for six months. This what he provided to numerous *"San Felese"*. My father being one of these. My uncle was a conduit for many people to make a new life in *"The Lucky Country"*.

The house was located in Janet Street, Five Dock Sydney Australia (which later was subsumed by The Department of Education, knocked down and become the oval for "Drummoyne Boys' High School", (which later was sold off to build townhouses on). The job was at *"Lysaght Wire and Steel Foundry"* located in Abbotsford, Sydney NSW.

My father often told me that:

"I went from Heaven to Hell!"

This is what my father would often tell me of his experience when first arriving in Australia.

The *"Hell"* he was referring to was working in a factory for ten hours a day, five days a week, without ever seeing the sun! There was plenty of *"overtime"* for anyone who had the *"balls"* to work even more! My father had very big *"balls"*! If this was not *"Hell"* enough, his work was in the foundry section, where molten metal (of temperatures exceeding five hundred degrees Celsius), were poured into moulds.

This was truly ***"HELL"*** for my father!

As part of his immigration entry requirements, he had to attend English classes two nights a week, Tuesday and Thursday from 6pm to 9pm, every week. My father was almost completely illiterate in his first language (having only six months of education in Italian). So, this was a Herculean feat for him, but he persevered and his English was actually not too bad……when he wanted use it!

Being alone meant that he a freedom to do whatever he wanted. The only other time he had this level of freedom was when was conscripted into the Italian Army in 1939 to fight the Allies. Italy was on the *"Other Side"* with the Germans early on in WWII, where he was sent to Bologna to *"peel"* potatoes. Then ran away and fled when the Germans came! He was actually classified as a traitor until Italy jumped the fence and joined the Americans to fight against the Germans *(but that's another story)*.

With his best friend, *Compare Jerry Di Giacomo (Compare is Godfather, Jerry is my Godfather)*, they terrorised the streets of Five Dock and Drummoyne much to the chagrin and annoyance of my uncle. Nevertheless, he was able to accumulate enough money for a deposit on a house in Five Dock, ready for us to move straight into when we arrived from Italy. If nothing else, my father was a very proud man!

Everything had changed for him. Even his name was changed. He was no longer called Giuseppe. He was now Joe!

When we arrived from Italy my father was on Christmas holidays from *Lysaght* and had found a temporary job at *Toohey's Brewery* located in *Mary Street, Surry Hills*, where *The World Square* is now. *(It moved in 1975 to its current location in Nyrang Street Lidcombe)*.

He liked it so much that he quickly resigned from *Lysaght* and went to work at *Toohey's* all of his working life until he retired in 1989.

My father was an angry and bitter man. He was very dominating and very violent (physically and psychologically) and abusive both to my mother and to me.

When I was about six years old, he hit me with a belt. I still have the scars on my back. I don't remember the situation but I do remember tears running down my face and being angry as hell. I swore to him that I would get him back at him one day. I would enact my revenge.

I did *(but that's another story)*!

He was a doctor, prosecutor, judge and jury all in one. He could and would determine the fate of a person instantly. There was no need for elaborate court cases or the presumption of being innocent before being proven guilty. He could tell is someone was guilty with absolutely no information or evidence. Let's face it, everyone is guilty of something. He didn't need evidence. That was all irrelevant. He just knew. It was like a sixth sense.

They were guilty!

Case closed.

Hang them!

If you had facial hair, long hair, matted hair, coloured hair, sculptured hair, no hair, unkept hair, dishevelled clothes, dirty clothes, torn clothes, skimpy clothes, no clothes, tattoos, body piercings, too much jewellery, hippies, bodgies, bikies, atheists, non-Catholics and anyone coloured, were all guilty!

Most people from southern Italy were very superstitious and practised weird rituals and my father was no different. These included doing things by the phases of the moon such as: cutting his hair, toe nails, making wine, killing animals, pruning trees which were all done when the moon was waning. Planting seeds or anything connected to growth was done when the moon was waxing.

He also had the crazy idea that he could tell if someone was gossiping about him. He would Say *"tange nu frisce in da vrecchio"*, I have a whistle in my ear. If it was in the left ear, it was bad, if it was in the right ear, it was good. Then he would say *"counte, counte"*, count until he would say stop, when the whistling stopped, then using that number, say 6, he would count to the 6th letter of the alphabet "F". He would search for a person's name or *supronomo* that started with "F", after a few seconds he would shout out *"Fresce"*, he was convinced that this person was talking about him!

He also had some great sayings which just don't do them justice when they are translated into English:

- *"Sere sere, vadgnio, vadgnio. A tripe mia stia sampre diggiona!"*,
  (Hill, hill, valley, valley. My stomach is always empty!)
  This was said after a hearty meal, especially if someone asked you if the meal was satisfying and you were full.
  (Apparently, it's about a goat!)

- *"Qunada a borsa a borsa! Quanda a bovila a bovila!"*
  (When you go for bags, you go for bags! When you go for butterflies, you go for butterflies!)
  This was said when you are doing something or going somewhere and some point there is a new choice or direction presented to you.

- *"Voglio andare a postare una lettera!"*
  (I want to go and post a letter!)
  This was said straight after lunch when you wanted to be excused to go to the toilet.

- *"Primo de domanini!"*
  (Before tomorrow!)
  This was said when you very EXCITED about doing something and couldn't wait.)

- *"Posse suspirare!"*
  (I can breathe!)
  This was said when he came back to his house @ 16 Elizabeth Street, Five Dock.

- *"Non Posse suspirare!"*
  (I cannot breathe!)
  This was said when he was at someone else's house!

- *"Casa mia bella!"*
  (My beautiful house!)
  This was said when he came back to his house in Elizabeth Street, Five Dock.

He loved his house in Elizabeth Street, Five Dock!

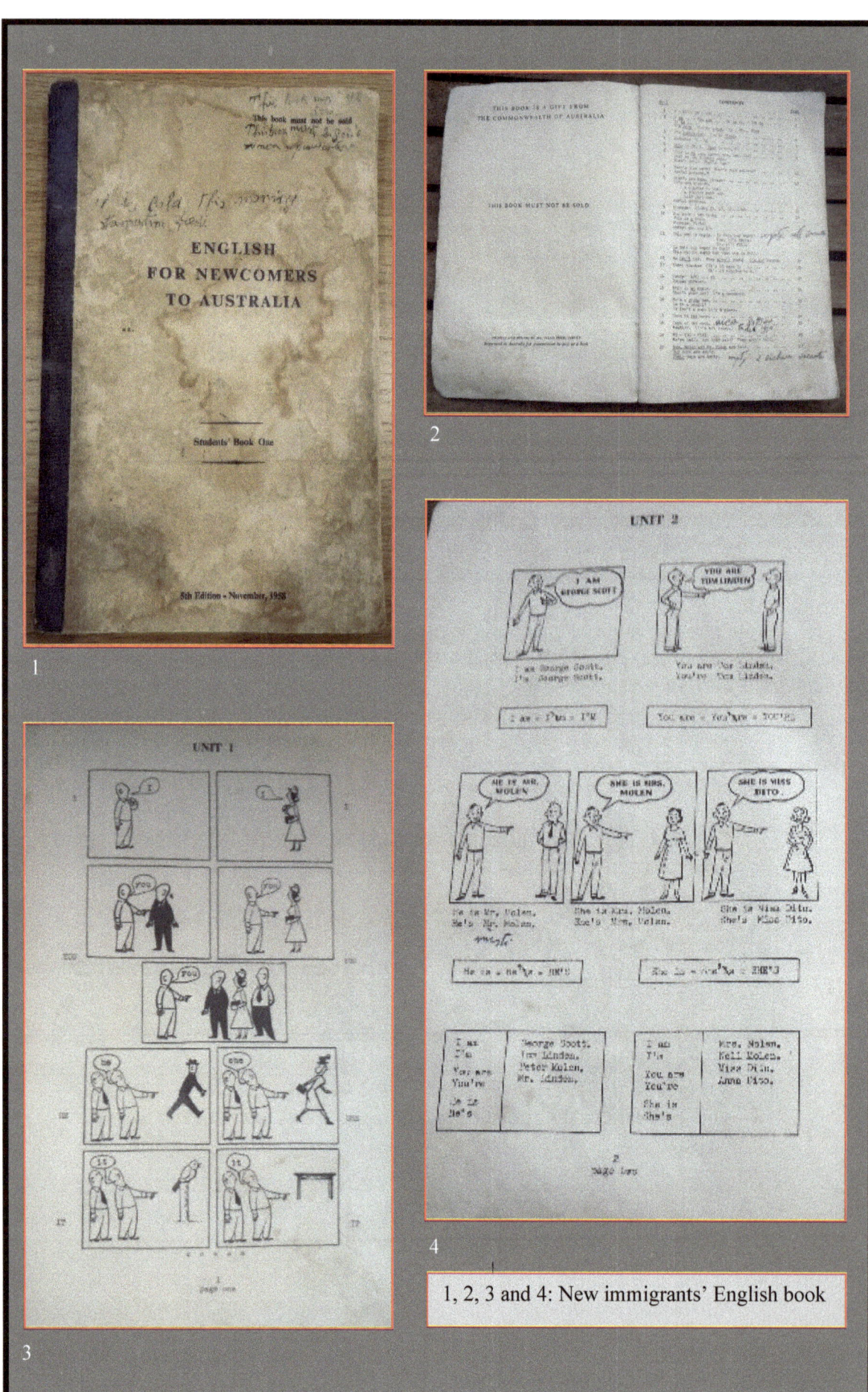

1, 2, 3 and 4: New immigrants' English book

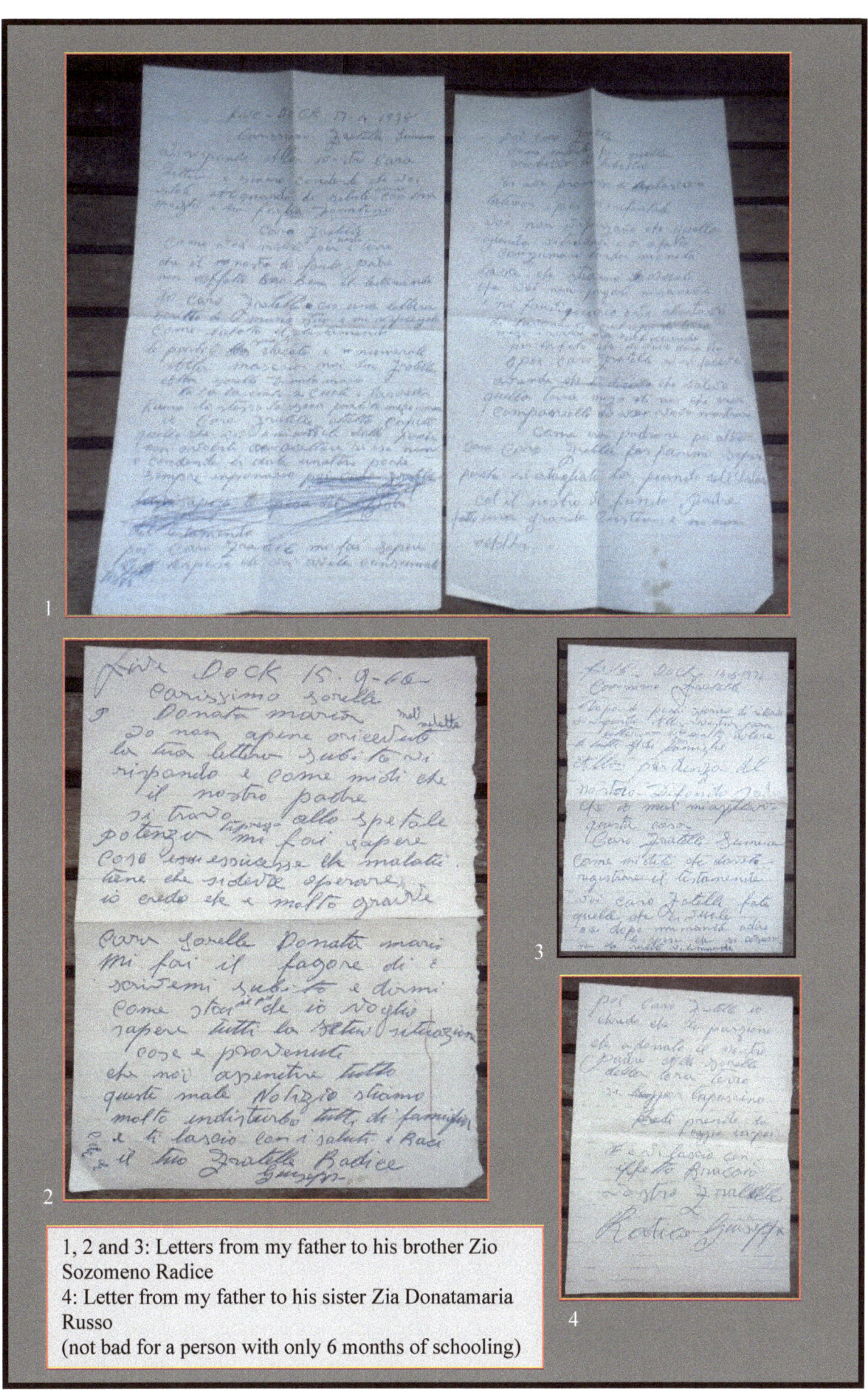

1, 2 and 3: Letters from my father to his brother Zio Sozomeno Radice
4: Letter from my father to his sister Zia Donatamaria Russo
(not bad for a person with only 6 months of schooling)

1: Father in backyard
2: Father in front yard

All photos 1960-1964

3: Cousin Joe Carnevale, Zia Laura, Father and Great Uncle Giuseppe Carnevale
4: Great Uncle, Uncle Michaele and Zia Laura in front of the new Chrysler Valiant
5: Zia Laura and Zio Michaele
6: Great Uncle Giuseppe and Cousin Joe

Chapter 6: School Days

My first day at Five Dock Primary school was a very traumatic experience for my brother and I. My mother's cousin who was supposed to take us didn't come so we went off by ourselves, both having absolutely no English knowledge at all.

The school was not far from our house, about a five-minute walk away.
Nick was placed into Year six of Primary School, a separate building, but still in the same grounds. I was placed in kindergarten.

There was only one simple rule in the school playground in those days and probably is still today; *"bully or be bullied!"* I was bullied! I was: *"pantsed"*, when the boy behind you in the assembly line pulled down you shorts exposing you oversized y-fronted underpants,

- called names *"Vito Mosquito"*,
- called a *"Wog"*, a derogatory term for Southern Europeans,
- ridiculed and laughed at because of the food that my mother had made for my lunch. My lunch usually consisted of two thick slices of crusty Vienna bread, filled with either, salami, Mortadella, cheese, spinach, eggplants, zucchini, onions, garlic, anchovy, capsicums, mozzarella, frittata *(Italian omelette)*.

Gourmet sandwiches today but not in 1965.

These were NOT the fillings the other kids had, which consisted predominantly of two slices of "Tip Top" white bread, containing either peanut butter or vegemite or both, all in a neat container!
Now as you can imagine, by lunchtime, my sandwiches, wrapped in butchers' paper and in my school bag for over 3 hours, had started to ferment. The smell when exposed to air was quite ripe. The other kids curious to see what I had for lunch had a field day! They fell about laughing and shouting; *"Oooooow, what is that? Are those worms? Is that shit that you're eating?"*
"Wog, Wog, Wog, Wog, Wog!"

So there was only one thing to do…… …..throw my lunch in the bin!

I went without lunch!

Oh, how I wished to have lunch like everyone else!

One lunchtime, my teacher who was on playground duty, noticed that I wasn't eating, she might have even seen me throw my food into the bin. I'm not sure. She came over to where I was sitting and asked me where my lunch was, of course, I couldn't answer. I could see in her eyes and face that she didn't require an answer, so she walked off and a few minutes later came back and handed me a meat pie.

My very first meat pie ever!

I loved it!

Nick took no shit from anyone and he quickly asserted his position in the primary school. The head bully picked on him one day but Nick was not one to back down from a fight and quickly jumped on him, put his ear into his mouth and bit it. The boy was screaming and crying and there was blood everywhere!

My parents were called to the school. The boy and his ear were all fine.

Nick was NEVER bullied again!

The story quickly spread throughout the entire school.

I was safe………until he left for high school! Then I was fucked again!

Since I was not a fighter like Nick, the only option I felt I had for me not to be bullied was……. to be THE BEST! To be the best and excel at everything, both academic and sport!

To be the smartest, the fastest, the most creative!

Whatever it was I become SUPER competitive!

I took no prisoners!

No one stood in my way!

And I SUCEEDED!

I was no longer bullied! I was looked up to and admired!

Respected even!

My best friend was *Phillip Berry*, "*a true-blue Aussie*". He lived on *James Street*, the second house up from the water at *"Hen and Chicken Bay"*, Five Dock. He had four older brothers *(all with long, straight black hair)* and an older sister. His father worked *(I never knew what he did)* but his mother did not and stayed at home.

I loved his family! I often would wish that I was his brother and had been born into his family! They were the complete opposite to my family and everything we did. They seemed normal to me and we were not!

They loved Rugby league and he was a very good player. He was selected for the Western Suburbs region and for the state. I was just as good but was not allowed to play. My father was never one for sport, seeing it as waste of time and money, especially Rugby League, which he thought was way too rough and that I would get hurt.

Phillip supported *"Canterbury Bankstown"*, (in fact his whole family did), which at the time were called *"The Berries"*, which explains why he went for them *(today they are called "The Bulldogs", "The Berries" was obviously too soft for the modern era)*. They were also my team for a short time until I started supporting the *"St George Dragons"* or simply *"The Dragons"* or *"Saints"*. Probably because their colours were red and white *(red was my favourite colour)* or because all they had on the jersey was a big, red "V" *(V for Vito)!*

I was a *"Latch-Key Kid"*, both my parents went off to work very early in the mornings and arrived late in the afternoons, so my mother tied the house key around the shoulder strap of my singlet and was left to fend on my own in the mornings and afternoons.

My mother's first job was as a *"piece-meal"* worker at *"Kolotex"*, a hosiery mill in *George street, Leichhardt*, owned by the *Kornmehl Family*. Basically, it was a *"sweat-shop"* where women worked on machines or sowed by hand. My mother sowed by hand. The more items you sowed the more bonuses your team got. All the sowers were women! All the "leading-hands" & bosses were men! They pushed the women very hard and were very authoritarian and competitive. The women were not allowed to talk to each other or take breaks.

She started work at 7:30am in the morning and finished at 4:30pm in the afternoon with a ten-minute break for morning and afternoon tea and half an hour for lunch. They had to "bundy on and off" each morning and afternoon. They would be docked pay if they arrived late or left early. A hooter went off at the start and finish of the day. It was very rigid! *("Bundying on and off" was very common in labouring factories, where workers had a time-sheet which had to be stamped on, at the start of the day and stamped off, at the end of the day. If you did not get it stamped, you did not get pay. If you were late ten minutes or left 10 minutes early, your pay was cut, "docked" by half an hour!)*

My mother HATED it!

This is the Kolotex factory in George Street, Leichhardt, taken in the late 1960s at 10.55am. The Time Clock ("Bundy Clock") is on the left-hand corner wall.

All photos circa 1967-1968

1: Mother with her sister, Zia Donatamaria Tronnolone from Adelaide
2: Zia Donatamaria, father and mother in the backyard of the house in Five Dock
3: Zio Antonio Tronnolone, Nick, Zia, mother, cousin Mary, father (back row) (front row) cousin Vito, me & cousin Pat
4: Zio Antonio, Zia Donatamaria, mother and father next to the old garage
5: Nick, Mary, Vito, me and Pat
6: Zio Michaele, Zia Laura, mother, me, father and Nick

Mornings were particularly stressful for me as I didn't know when to go to school. I was in a dilemma: If I went TOO early, I would be the only one there, if I went TOO late, I would have missed valuable time playing with my friends. I neither had a watch or could tell the time. So, I devised a simple strategy: our backyard and driveway was made of concrete, I would run and jump, if I landed in a square: time to go, if I landed on the dividing line between tow squares: it was not time to go.

The method seemed to work very well!

The driveway separated our house with our nextdoor neighbour's house and there was no fence separating the two houses until the backyard started. *"The Wade"* family lived there until the early 1970s. They had two children (a boy and girl) who were both sent to boarding school. *"Mrs Wade"* stayed at home and *"Mr Wade"* went to work *(I never really knew what he did, although I think he was a lawyer)*.

Their kitchen window was very low and overlooked our driveway and since there was no fence dividing the two properties, I was able to reach up and talk to Mrs Wade when she was doing the cooking for dinner. Many an afternoon was spent standing at her window talking to her. I loved *"Mrs Wade"*. She was kind, warm, intelligent supportive and full of love for everyone. She would encourage me to study and be creative and I learnt a lot from her. In fact, my interest in art, especially drawing and painting, was started by her.

One day she gave me a set of watercolour paints which I loved so much and quickly started painting all sorts of things. I remember painting the side of her house with the kitchen window and *"Mrs Wade"* at it, looking out. She loved that painting so much so that I gave it to her and she hung it up on her kitchen wall, directly opposite the window, so I could see it when I looked in.

I was SO proud!

I wanted to be part of her family too!

Our house had an outside toilet *"outside dunny", ("dunny" is Australian slang for toilet)*, it still does today. It has no electricity, so it was a very traumatic experience for me when I had to go to the toilet in the middle of a dark night. Opposite the toilet was a very old, huge wooden barn/workshop/garage, with massive wooden old doors. I would try to keep it in as much as possible but eventually I would succumb and rush outside. I would try to be as fast as I could but nevertheless it was always a very scary. I always thought that I could see shapes in the shadows and darkness through the barn door which sometimes was left open. Sometimes I would close my eyes and pretend that I could transport myself back into the warmth and safety of my bed. Unfortunately, I could not and had to run back as fast as I could, back to my bed. I was very terrified.

On Christmas day 1965, *"Mr Wade"* completely filled the toilet up with toys! Everyone was amazed! My father was ANGRY! He quickly blamed me for being too friendly with the Wade family. Mr Wade came over noticing that my father was unhappy and said, *"Joe, Joe, these gifts are not for you, they are for your son. Don't be angry! We want to give him presents because it's Christmas time and because we want to!"*

My father begrudgingly accepted their kindness but he always had this feeling he would owe them! He always had this feeling of obligation if someone gave him a gift or was invited to something. He did not understand the act and pleasure in giving or in receiving.

My father never liked getting gifts!

The best and largest present was a red scooter.

I loved that scooter.

I now had wheels!

I was mobile!

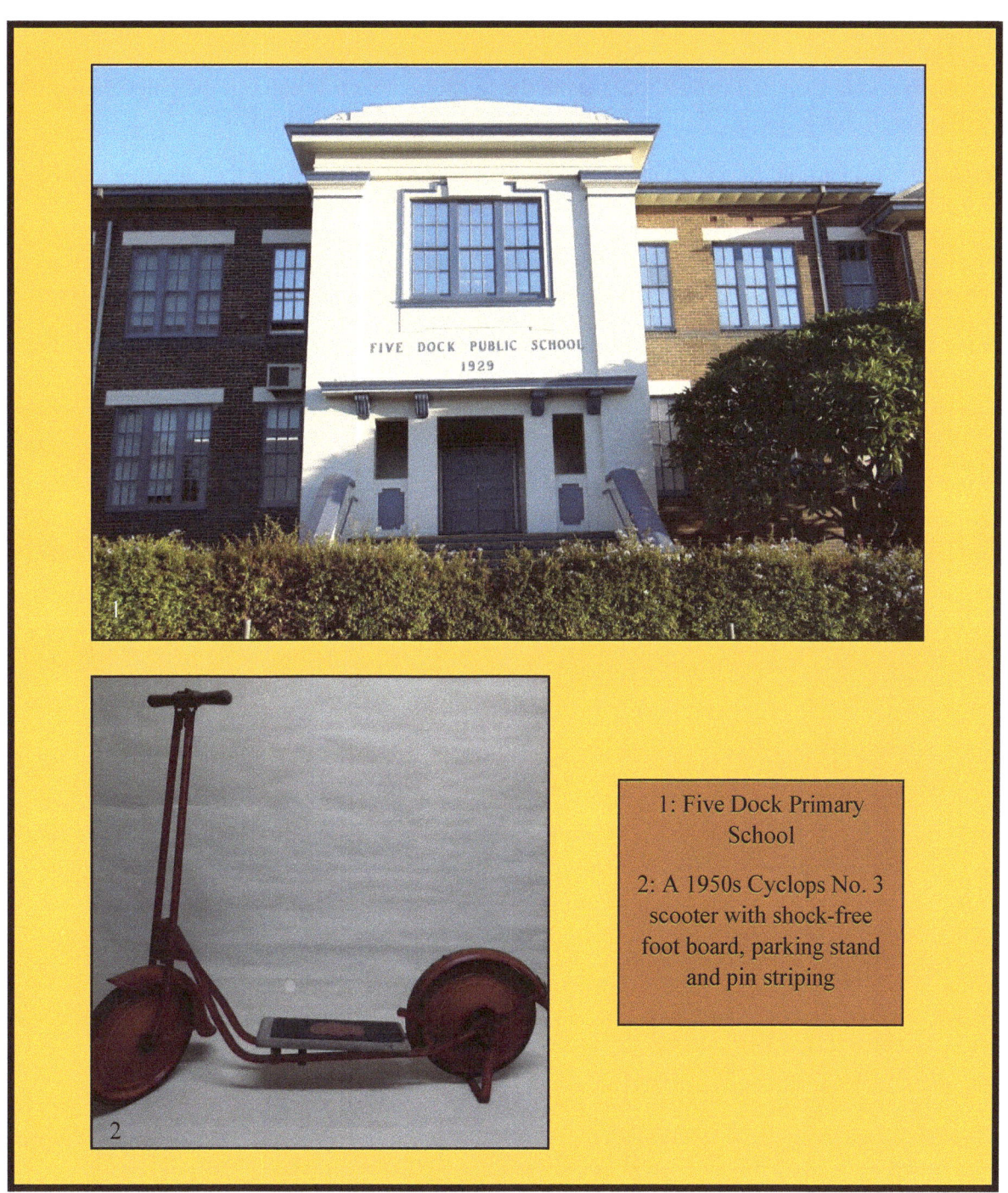

1: Five Dock Primary School

2: A 1950s Cyclops No. 3 scooter with shock-free foot board, parking stand and pin striping

Chapter 7: My Life with Chickens!

The first thing my parents did in the Five Dock house was build a chook pen at the back of the yard. My father was not a skilled builder, in fact, he was awful with the use of his hands. So, the chook pen was a mix of chicken wire as an enclosure, a wooden X-framed door covered with chicken wire, corrugated iron sheets as a roof and walls (with some hay on the floor) where the chickens could shelter and lay their eggs and the rest had a dirt floor. Nothing too flash.

It was my job to feed and collect the eggs in the morning, and to clean out the chicken pen in the evening. This involved picking up the chicken poo! I hated this job!

Once a month I would be forced to go to *"The Fresh Food Markets"* in the city on a Saturday morning at 4:30am with my dad to buy live chickens. (He liked fresh food!).

The markets were located where the old *"Entertainment Centre"* was. The markets were demolished to make way for it and now, it has also been demolished! Who knows what is

being built to replace it. That place has a lot of memories and history but who will remember and tell its story?

1 & 2: The Sydney fresh food markets, Haymarket, Sydney

The markets were a hive of activity, although I hated getting up at such an ungodly hour.

There was a cacophony of sounds as you entered the huge archway entrance of the building which was basically a huge covered space with all the different stalls set up in rows.

"Pannini! Si magna!", an Italian man with a tray of bread rolls stuffed with all manner of delights would walk around shouting, for anyone to buy. It was early morning and everyone was hungry (especially me). He made a rip-roaring trade. Although, my father never bought me one of those eye-wateringly, delicious *"pannini"*!

My father knew exactly where to go and he didn't waste any time. The live animals, such as turkeys, ducks, rabbits, were located in wire cages at the back wall of the markets nearest to the Dixon Street end.

He would buy five or six chickens, depending on the size and price. My father always haggled over the price. He had a price in his head and that was it. Nothing could dislodge him. He would haggle over ten cents. He was the best haggler I have ever seen. He loved to haggle!

We would then place the live chickens into a banana cardboard box, which had holes around it, was waxed for added strength and had a lid which we had brought with us. He had tied a rope around both ends which acted as a strap for us to hold. My father on one end, I on the other, we walked up to central bus stop, carrying our load of chickens to take the Number 437 or 438 bus back to Five Dock!

Buses in those days had conductors to collect your fare, so we had to be very careful because it was not allowed to take live animals onto a bus, especially chickens.

We would sit on the long, rear bench seat if it was a single decker bus (there were also double-decker buses) and put the box containing the live chickens underneath it.

This was an extremely traumatic and stressful bus ride!

On one particular Saturday morning, not only were the chickens making noises and pooing in the box, with its accompanying smells bad enough but they somehow managed to jump out of the box and fly throughout the bus. Luckily for us it was still very early in the morning and the bus was empty. The chickens were making a last desperate bid for freedom, aware of the fate that awaited them, which was not going to be good!

They pooed throughout the bus, on the seats, on the floor, on the windows, wherever they could they pooed! It was complete bedlam. My father and I running manically up and down the aisle trying to catch them and put them back into their box. We were able to finally recapture the escapees but not without a fierce battle. Those chickens did not want to be captured!

The conductor was very sympathetic and let us off with a warning, telling us not to bring live animals in a box onto a bus. That it was not allowed and against the law!

It was in these moments that I wished I had the superpower of *"invisibility"*!

It would have come in very handy for me!

> ***DISCLAIMER: Reader be aware: the next section contains detailed, graphic information about animal cruelty and could cause PERMANENT psychological damage! It did to me!***

When we arrived home, which usually was around 6:00am, it was time to kill the chickens!

Once we arrived home, there was not time for breakfast! First we had to kill, pluck and wash the chickens. This was a family bonding activity! My father, my mother and myself. My brother would be excused from this activity!

The killing of the chickens was a particularly harrowing experience for me for a variety of reasons, least of which was smelling my father's farts! This just added to the whole macabre, sensory situation.

The chicken was placed in between my father's thighs, with its head hanging out. My job was to hold the chicken's legs, at an elevated forty-five degree angle, behind his back, up his backside, so that its head was lower than its feet. This was a very uncomfortable position for me because my face was almost at the same level as my father's bum (hence the farting).

With his left hand, my father would grab the chickens head and beak, with his right hand he would pluck some of the feathers from the back of its head and then with a very sharp knife cut along the ridge of the head and neck, slowly allowing the warm blood to drain of its body and into a bowl into which it was being collected.

The forty-five degree angle of elevation was extremely important in the process because it allowed gravity to drain the blood from its body while its heart was still beating and pumping the blood around its body only to be released into the bowl.

The chicken would put up a struggle, of course, but it was no match for my father's massive thighs which clenched tight around its body like a vice!

Quite often the chicken would poo at this time!

It would take about five minutes before the chicken's body became limp and we knew it was dead!

This was repeated for the remainder of the chickens and placed on a pile.

On one particular occasion, from the lifeless bodies piled on top of one another, to our utter astonishment and disbelief, a body sprang to life in front of our eyes. It sprang up as if life tried one last time to reassert itself and defeat Death. It ran around the backyard in circles, as if in a frenzied dance, with its head flopping from side to side and just as suddenly as it arose, it collapsed.

Death had won!

I guess this is where the saying; *"running around like a headless chook"* comes from!

The next step was to pluck the chickens which involved removing all the feathers. Whilst the chickens were being slaughtered a large pot of water was being boiled over an open wood fire. This was all down outside at the back of the yard in the BBQ area. The chickens were dunked into the boiling water for a few moments, pulled out and the feathers quickly plucked. There was a particular smell of the warm, wet feathers which I can still smell now.

Once all the chickens were plucked it was now time to open them up, remove the internal organs clean and wash them. Nothing was thrown away. The heart, liver, the giblet was opened up peeled of its inner lining, the intestines were split open and thoroughly washed, the bile sack was carefully cut away from the liver, this was a very delicate process because if the sack containing the bile, (which was a green colour and poisonous), was broken and contaminated the liver, it was no longer edible.

The chickens were then hung up to dry, cut up into pieces and put into the freezer.

The warm, collected blood quickly congealed from a deep burgundy turning into a deep purple black colour. This was set aside which would be later boiled for a couple of minutes in salty water. This now turned into a gun metal grey colour with holes throughout it like a sponge. This was set aside to cool, and then cut up into chunks and fried in olive oil, garlic, onions, potatoes, red capsicums and any other vegetables or also as a frittata.

This was then eaten with crusty pane di casa.

This was our breakfast!

It was *"molto deliciouso"*, very delicious!

Three vintage buses

Chapter 8: Sydney: *A Simpler Time!*

Sydney was a much more innocent and simpler place in the 1960s. On Saturdays *ALL* shops closed at midday and night shopping…forget about it! Of course, *EVERYTHING* was closed on Sundays! Sunday was reserved for family!

My father worked most of his life at '*Toohey's Brewery*', in fact from 1964 to 1991 (27 years). First in Mary Street, Surry Hills and then it moved to Nyrang Street, Auburn. He worked in the cask yard all the time.

He loved his job!

During his 4 week annual holidays he would also find another job. This was not allowed but he would make up a story *(usually saying that he came from Adelaide)*. Some of the places that I remember that he worked in were; *"Don's Small Meats"* in Leichhardt, where he used to bring home lots of ham, salami, prosciutto, Devon etc. and *"CSR" (a sugar refinery)* in Pyrmont, where he would bring home 4 gallon glass bottles of pure alcohol *(Ethanol)*, which my mother would use to make her own homemade spirits using flavourings such as mandarin, cherry, orange, lemon, Licorice etc.

My father also tried to work as much overtime as possible to earn more money. Overtime was paid at penalty rates, which was time and a half, double time or even triple time. This was very desirable. He worked overtime most evenings (paid at time and a half) and half a day some Saturdays (paid at double time). Sundays (paid at triple time) was very rare.

When he worked on a Saturday and he was in good mood, he would bring back half a cooked pigs head (boiled by the butcher). The pig's head was completely cut vertically in half. Half a brain, one eye, one ear, half a tongue etc. He bought this at *"Caminiti's Butcher"* the corner of Great North Road and Henry Street Five Dock, opposite where the old post office used to be. *"Caminiti's"* is still there, now run by the son. The post office is no longer there and the building lies empty and abandoned!

Butchers in those days all had saw dust on the floor to collect any blood that was dropped. All the meat was wrapped up in butcher's paper and everything was fresh.

The pigs' heads were piled in a heap in the window of the butcher's shop and they were very cheap. When my father arrived home with the pig's head wrapped up in butcher's paper. We knew that he had had a good day and that we were going to have good afternoon.

He spread it out on the red Formica kitchen table and red plastic covered chairs, like a proud hunter returning from his kill. We all sat around the boiled head devouring it like Vikings.

We were one family in this moment!

Everyone was happy!

The pig's head was *"molto deliciouso"*!

After having our fill and being satiated with our meal, we all went off for an afternoon siesta.

The house was quiet!

The house at this moment was a *"home"*!

We also had fresh bread *(Vienna, pane di casa)* delivered to us every weekday and seven loaves on a Friday to last the whole weekend. We loved our bread. We ate bread with everything, even with pasta, especially with pasta, when we would dunk the crusty bread into the *"ragu"*, wiping every last bit from the plate. We were big eaters!

Once a week *"Giovanni a'Spezza"* would come around his small trunk laden with all manner of delicacies, eggs, pasta, cheese, salami, fruit, he had it all. He owned a grocery store in Haberfield, the neighbouring suburb, but once a week he would drive around, selling his produce to Italians. He was a short, old, balding, grey-haired man. What made him unusual though, was that he only had one arm! His left arm had been cut off at the shoulder. He was able to manage very well with just his right arm, which I found very impressive. I never asked him directly what had happened to his left arm, but the story that was told was that he had tried to escape from a prison camp in the war and that the Germans cut off his arm as an example to the other prisoners. I think it worked!

We also had fresh milk home delivered every morning by the *"milkman"*.

We bought our first black and white television set in 1968. It was a very exciting time. The TV was a modular, top of the range Kriesler 36" CRT and was the centrepiece of the lounge room. It changed my life FOREVER! Nothing was ever the same after getting the TV!

My favourite TV shows were:

- Bonanza (Lorne Green, Purnell Roberts, Dan Blocker, Michael Landon)
- The Mod Squad (Clarence William III, Peggy Lee,
- Mission Impossible
- The Big Valley (Barbara Stynwycke, Lee Majors)
- Batman *(Adam West & Burt Ward)*
- Bewitched *(Elizabeth Montgomery)*
- I Dream of Jeannie *(Larry Hagman & Barbara Eden)*
- Green Acres *(Eva Gabor, Eddie)*
- Petticoat Junction
- My Three Sons
- The Many Loves of Dobie Gillis *(Dwayne Hickman)*
- Gilligan's Island *(Bob Denver)*
- I Spy *(Bill Crosby, Robert Culp)*
- The Man from U.N.C.L.E. *(Robert Vaughn, David McCallum)*
- The Saint *(Roger Moore)*
- Cheyenne
- Daniel Boone *(Fess Parker)*
- Jim Bowie
- The Phantom Agents *(10:00am on a Saturday morning)*
- Dangerman *(Patrick McGoohan)*

- Prisoner (Patrick McGoohan)
- Thunderbirds
- Captain Scarlet
- The Waltons
- The Beverly Hillbillies
- Star Trek *(William Shatner & Leonard Nimoy)*
- Maverick
- Kung Fu *(David Carradine)*
- Brian Henderson's Bandstand *(at 6:30pm on a Saturday night straight after the 6 O'clock news)*
- The Bobby Limb Variety Show *(at 7:320pm on a Friday night)*
- Reg Lindsay's Country and Western Hour *(at 1:00pm on a Saturday arvo)*
- Nock and Kirby's (Joe the Gadget Man)
- Wrestling *(at 12:00 midday on a Saturday)*
- Sunday afternoon Football *(they only televised the 2nd half and the commentators were Ron Casey and Rex "Moose" Mossop)*

My favourite cartoons were:

- The Flintstones
- Marine Boy
- Prince Planet
- Rocky and Bullwinkle
- Superman
- Spiderman
- Marvel Super Heroes
- Gigantor
- The Magilla Gorilla Show
- Fractured Fairy Tales

We bought it from *"John Whitford's Family Store"*, in Five Dock owned by *"John Whitford"*. In fact, we bought everything from *"Whitford's"* because it had EVERYTHING! You could buy whatever you wanted there, furniture, electrical and whitegoods. It's still there today as *"John Whitford's Electrical Discount Store"* run by his sons. This was where I used to see and closely study my father's incredible haggling skills. He was a master at it. It was at the same time beautiful and excruciatingly painful to watch and experience. Truly *"A Dance Macabre"*! He would only negotiate with John himself and John was your typical Aussie bloke, very kind, warm, inviting and honest to the core. The final stages of the dance were very beautiful. John would put out his hand and say, *"Ok Joe, you have a deal!"* and there would be handshakes and big smiles all round. *John Whitford* was a great bloke!

"Whitford's" was located on *"Great North Road"*, the main road through Five Dock (it has just recently been bulldozed to make way for the new "Lightrail"). I never understood what was so *"Great"* about it and it wasn't even that long, running only about three kilometres from Parramatta Road at its south to Abbottsford Point at its north. Along it, was Five Dock shopping centre in which I would spend a lot of my time. One of my favourite stores was *"Coles Variety Store"*, located at the very southern end of the shopping centre. It no longer

exists! The layout was very simple, one large counter in the centre of the store which contained an aisle for the sales staff to be in, broken half way down the store, creating two walking aisles and four rows of merchandise.

This is where I bought my first LP record of *"The Beatles Greatest Hits"*. I was very excited and rushed to play it on our new record player that my brother had proudly bought for the household. When I put it on you can imagine my disappointment when, it was NOT The Beatles but *"Bert Kaempfert plays The Beatles Greatest Hits on piano"*!

One of the most inspirational, amazing and transformative events for me, that would set my imagination racing for the rest of my life, occurred on a cold and wet July morning. I was in 4th class of primary school and the whole school was ushered into the school hall to sit down on the cold wooden floor and watch a very small black and white television screen. I remember it clearly. I was seated quite close, about four rows from the front, so I had an excellent view of the screen. We sat there from 9:00 am and even had recess and lunch there. We were not allowed to go anywhere. This was a very big occasion. It was a world changing occasion. The date was July 21st, 1969. *"The Moon Landing!"*

Then it happened, about 1:00pm. I watched in utter astonishment and amazement, Neil Armstrong climb gingerly down the ladder of "The Eagle" to be the first human being EVER to set foot on another world in or solar system. When he took his first steps on the surface of The Moon, in the *"Sea of Tranquility"* and spoke those now awe-inspiring words:

"One small step for man, one giant leap for mankind!".

Those words, spoken by Neil Armstrong, still now, bring a chill and a tingle down my spine!

I felt one with humanity!

I knew then, humans could achieve ANYTHING! That even with all the hatred and wars in the world, I felt that if we could achieve this amazing feat, we could, one day overcome these as well.

I was filled with joy and happiness.

I was ten years old!

I watched as the camera panned the desolate lunar landscape. Enthralled by the achievement and pondered at what they must have been feeling and thinking as they watched planet Earth from afar, possibly to never return home. Like other previous adventurers and explorers that discovered new worlds on Earth, they
had ventured where no human had EVER been before and in so doing risked their own lives for the advancement of human dreams, curiosity and knowledge.

This started my lifelong interest in:
- *science fiction,*
- *space,*
- *space exploration*
- *space colonization,*
- *technology,*

- *extra-terrestrials,*
- *aliens,*

> "Space, the final frontier
> These are the voyages of the Starship Enterprise.
> Its five years mission,
> To explore strange new worlds,
> To seek out new life,
> And new civilizations,
> To boldly go where no man has gone before!"
>
> "Star Trek Classic"
> Words spoken by William Shatner
> (Captain James T. Kirk of the Starship "Enterprise")

- *alien lifeforms,*
- *cosmology,*
- *philosophy,*
- *The meaning in/of life,*
- *Eastern philosophy and religions,*
- *Synchronicity,*
- *Singularity,*
- *augmentation,*
- *cybernetics,*
- *HuBots,*
- *Artificial Intelligence (AI) and*
- *artificial lifeforms!*

I became enthralled by space, science fiction. I began to read science fiction, my favourite author was and still is today, *"John Wyndham"*. To me, he was the *"father"* of science fiction. Most of the greatest and most iconic themes, that have been used over and over again, in science fiction, came from his imagination! *"The Day of the Triffids"*, *"The Midwich Cuckoos"*, *"The Trouble with Lichen"*, *"The Kraken Wakes"*, *"The Chrysalids"*, *"Chocky"*.

Christmas holidays were especially a bad time for me because they would invariably coincide with my father's four weeks annual leave. This meant doing work around the house such as painting, fixing the roof, fixing the fence, there always seemed something that my father would find to fix. I would be required to be on standby and be on call at a moment's notice. This could include hold the ladder whist he cleaned the gutters. This was particularly distressing because he would only wear shorts and if I ever looked up I got an eyeful of his testicles in all their wrinkled glory.

A VERY disturbing sight I assure you!

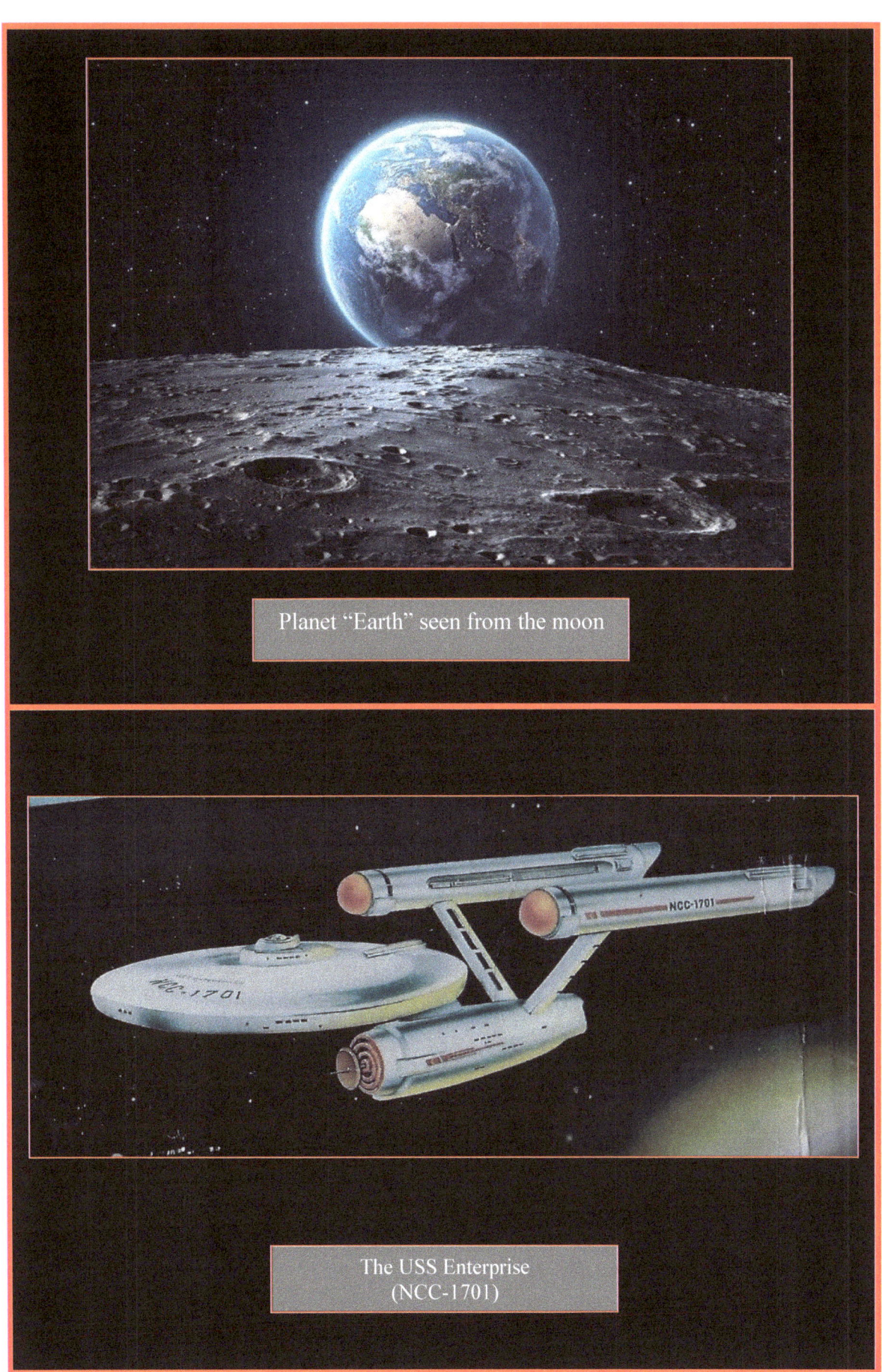

Planet "Earth" seen from the moon

The USS Enterprise
(NCC-1701)

Chapter 9: Death, God, Religion, Love and Masturbation!

What one has to understand is that my father was not a handyman. He could not fix things. What could be done in ten minutes would take him four hours and the end result was SHIT!

The other distressing thing was waiting for him to call out *"pilyama a'caussa!"*, *"get me the thing!"*. Panic would immediately set in. What thing? I would feverishly look around me looking to see if anything was obvious. There was not! I knew he was getting irritated.

My first girl I had a crush on was Gayle Saunders. She was the most beautiful girl to me. I drooled over her. We were both in the same class. She, on the other hand, favoured a new boy called Shane' who had just come to our school. I was so jealous of Shane. He was and had all the things that I didn't and wanted. He was an Aussie *(a "Skip")*, had straight, long blond hair and was very popular with the girls. They ALL drooled over him. I on the other hand was a *"Wog"*, had curly, short red hair with huge freckles all over my face. I always wished to be an Aussie, for long, straight black or blonde hair and be popular with girls. I was delusional!

One day I decided to let her know how I felt, so I decided to write her a note. A simple, brief and straight to the point note; *"I love YOU!"*. I gave it to Deborah Hatcher to deliver to Gayle. BIG mistake! Of course, she opened it, read it and passed it around to everyone else. Gayle was the last to receive it and when she did, she came straight over to me and was very angry, saying how could I do this to her. It was another one of those moments that I wished I could have had the superpower of *"Teleportation"*, so that I could instantaneously disappear!

I was NEVER lucky with *"LOVE"*!

Death was always a huge preoccupation for me. I never really knew why but I was always interested in what happened to you when you died. I'd lay awake in bed, in the darkness, sometimes with the sheets over my head and imagine myself dying. Was it like complete darkness? Was it like going to sleep and NEVER waking up? The only place to find answers to these questions was GOD!

I went to church, *"All Hallows Catholic Church"* in Five Dock every Sunday morning. Afterwards I went across the road to the Catholic Primary School, to attend Sunday School and learn teachings from the bible run by the nuns. I went for a couple of reasons not all spiritual and altruistic. It got me out of the house for at least 3 hours every Sunday from 7:00am to 10:00am. Nevertheless, I did become very religious and started to believe in a higher power, one who was omnipotent, listened to your problems and could fix them if you prayed and believed hard enough. I became very religious. I prayed all the time! I had many problems that needed fixing!

On one cold, bleak, windy and rainy school morning we were playing; *who could climb the netball posts the fastest*, in the enclosed bubbler and wash area. As always, I was very competitive and sprang onto the pole like a polecat eager to get to the top and touch the ring.

I was wearing shorts, I was about half way up when I started to experience very strange and unusual sensations in my penis as I was rubbing against the pole. I was very disturbed and shocked. In fact, I became quite disoriented. I reached the top and stayed there for a short time trying to figure what had just happened and get my breath back. I started to slide down and there was the sensation again. I decided that I had injured my dick somehow, but I could not tell anyone. I had to keep quiet! I prayed to God that I was alright!

That night in bed I decided to rub my dick and continue rubbing it. The sensation was like something I had never experienced before. It was FANTASTIC! The more I kept rubbing, the more I couldn't stop. Until, finally to my utter astonishment I felt like an explosion was taking over my whole body. I started shuddering, convulsing and then without warning a white fluid squirted out of my dick all over me! What the fuck had I done! Had I ruptured something? Oh God, I should've stopped when I had the chance! I was being punished! I had been bad! I turned to God! I prayed for God to save me because I was a sinner and I had sinned BIG time, to the point of rupturing some vital organ in my body! I was gonna DIE!

I told GOD that I would NEVER do that AGAIN!

But I was weak!

I succumbed to the DEVIL!

To TEMPTATION!

I was WEAK!

Every night I would succumb!

Every night I would REPENT!

I was ASHAMED at how weak I was!

One afternoon, Nick abruptly opened my bedroom door without knocking and caught me in the act. I started to cry at being caught. He just laughed and said *"Don't worry Vic, everyone does it! It's natural!"*.

With those few words, the world was back to normal again!

Vito
Circa 1974

Chapter 10: Family Time! A Bonding Time!
Just an Ordinary "Wog" Family

Weekends were 'Family Time". Time which was spent with my parents doing and making things.

I hated weekends!

I hated *"Family Time"!*

I would do anything to escape, even go to church!

This *"Family Time"* could be going to markets and getting chickens *(something I really loved……NOT!)*. Other activities which I also really looked forward to and loved, happened once a year. These included:

• Bottling Tomatoes

This happened in the month of January and could either take place on one day or it could be stretched out over a couple of weekends depending on the supply of overripe *"Roma"* tomatoes. They had to be *"Roma"* tomatoes because their shape was very important in this process, and a process it was indeed.

First just a few boxes of *"Roma"* tomatoes had to be brought from the markets, only about thirty boxes give or take. Then came the extremely laborious work of cutting up the *"Roma"* tomatoes into long strips. This was so they could be easily inserted into *"beer"* bottles which had a narrow mouth and neck!

Everybody was given a dedicated job. This was a production line. There were the cutters, who sliced up the *"Roma"* tomatoes. This was done on a large, thick wooden board. Then there were the bottle fillers, they put the slices of *"Roma"* tomatoes with leaves of *"basil"*, into the *"beer"* bottles. Lastly was the most important and difficult job of all……capping the bottles with a bottle cap.

Capping was done mechanically using a hammer and a cushion upon which the bottle was placed. The procedure was very simple, place the filled bottle of tomatoes onto the cushion, place the bottle top onto the bottle, a piece of wood with a metal cap was place onto the bottle top, hit the piece of wood with the hammer.

This was my job *(oh lucky me!)*

As you may realise this was fraught with danger!

The hitting had to be carried out with exact force. Use too much force and the bottle would shatter!

This was the worst-case scenario!

This was to be avoided at all costs!

Use not enough force and you would have to repeat the procedure but this time your confidence had been dented because of the previous failure, stress levels increased!

I was traumatised!

I guess I should have been proud to have been given such an important job. It probably meant I had the lowest number of breakages. I was the BEST!

It didn't make me feel any better.

Finally, when all the *"Roma"* tomatoes had been sliced and all the 200 or so bottles capped, it was time to sterilise the *"Roma"* tomatoes. This was done by heating a huge cauldron of water, putting the bottles into it and gently heating it, making sure the water never boiled because this could also shatter the bottles. I was not involved in this part *(thank God!)*.

These bottled tomatoes were used to make the most delicious pasta sauce!

• Making Wine

Making wine was another joyous event for me…. BUT especially for my father. This took place late March towards the end of summer, when the last and cheapest grapes became available. The whole process was very long and laborious. There was a pre-preparation week, the actual day of production and a post-production week of duties to be carried out! My job was to *"the goffer"*. That is, to do whatever the fuck my father wanted me to. Sometimes, I swear, he just got me to do things just for his own amusement because they made absolutely no fucking logical sense to me. I was basically his little slave to be ever ready, on standby for his call!!!

The pre-preparation week involved washing out all the wooden barrels, the grape press, the many containers, the glass flagons and setting up all the equipment ready for the BIG day.

The grapes had been ordered a couple of months earlier from *"Merlino"*, an Italian guy who was the middle man, organising the purchase, transport and delivery of the grapes to our home in a small ute. He would organise a semi-trailer laden with boxes of grapes from the Barossa Valley, South Australia to come to Five Dock for maybe twenty or thirty other families from the area. My father would always order the same quantity of boxes of grapes, twenty-five boxes of black grapes (usually Cabernet) and five boxes of white grapes (usually Waltham Cross), based on an average amount of wine produced per box and the size of his containers to store it in.

The actual day of wine making started early, about 5:30am, nothing unusual in that! My father was very keen to make sure that everything was prepared and ready for the delivery, and he had given strict instructions to *"Merlino il'cantiniere"* that he wanted first delivery. So, we were all put on *"battle-stations"*, ready for action at any moment!

When the ute finally arrived, everyone sprang into action. We all knew what to do. We had done this many times before. It was as if it was imprinted into our DNA. The boxes had to be unloaded and taken to the backyard of the house and pilled next to our nextdoor neighbour's *(Mr Brailley)* fence. The boxes were made of wood and so were quite heavy, containing on average anywhere between twenty or thirty kilograms of grapes. Later on, the boxes were made from polystyrene which made them slightly lighter. My father would at this stage check out the quality of the grapes and decide if the wine was going to be any good or not and whether they would produce a good yield. He would look at the size and quality of the grapes, if they were large and plump, this meant a good yield but very weak wine, too much water. If they were small and plump, this meant a small yield but a good alcohol content, optimal was 13% alcohol. If they were shrivelled and dried *"appassolito"*, this meant a very low yield but a very high alcohol content (possibly as high as 16%), this meant that the wine would be very strong and be very dark in colour. My father preferred a light, easy drinking wine rather than a heavy *"Shiraz"*.

Now the actual work started, crushing the grapes!

Initially, this was carried out using our feet in an old enamelled bathtub with claw feet, the ones that are now very sought after and very expensive, but actually this was a very inefficient method and was quickly replaced by a mechanical crushing machine. It consisted of a handle which turned two gears attached to two interlocking solid cylindrical gears which could be adjusted to vary the crushing strength for different sized grapes, to cater for small or large grapes which foot stomping could not. There were a lot of whole grapes left in the brew using feet. This was all but eliminated when using the crushing machine.

The machine was now placed onto the bathtub which collected the crushed grapes and brew. It could be filled with a couple of boxes and then the crushing started by turning the hand using brute, human strength. Initially, it was enough for gravity and the weight of the grapes to feed the cogs but most times, the grapes needed help to be fed into the cogs and this is where a closed fist or a large piece of wood came in handy.

My job alternated between carrying the boxes of grapes and filling the crushing machine to turning the handle of the crushing machine. Usually this turned into a competition to see who could crush a box of grapes the fastest. I of course was always the fastest. NO ONE could BEAT ME! I think I could crush a full box of grapes within thirty seconds! Pretty IMPRESSIVE!

The crushing of the grapes was actually the easy and mostly fun part of the day! We could crush all thirty boxes of grapes in about one hour!

The crushed grapes with all the juice was put into a very large wooden press (*"Il torquo"*), a mechanical separating machine. This was made from a very heavy, round metal base with a lip at some point on it is circumference and a metal pole attached in the middle which had a screw at the free end where a rotating head onto which a metal lever (basically a long metal pole) was inserted. Two wooden vertically slatted cages, with gaps between the slats, were then connected together to make a frame structure. This was filled with the crushed grapes and juice and then wooden blocks were placed on top, with the metal head wound to press down, allowing all the grape juice to flow out the lip but retain the grape skins, seeds and stalks inside. The grape juice was collected in a bucket and then transferred into a twenty-five litre or larger container made from wood or later from plastic, where the fermentation process would occur.

This kept on going until ALL the crushed grapes and juice were in the press and no more juice could be pressed out of them. This was grape juice, which was a cloudy purple red colour and very sweet and sticky. Next came the tedious parts of the process! ALL the stalks had to be removed from the crushed grapes and only the grape skins were left. Then a bucket of these grape skins was put into each of the containers of wine juice. Then a piece of fine wire mesh was placed over the mouth of the container. The reason for removing the grape stalks was that to put these into the grape juice would change the flavour of the wine and my father wanted an easy drinking wine, not too strong. He also prided himself in not adding any preservatives or stabilisers to the juice. He would proudly boast; *"Mio vino e tutti pure e natural! (My wine is totally pure and natural!)"*

The fermentation process of turning grape juice into wine had already started.

The wine containers had to be stirred regularly, at least a couple of times a day to assist and accelerate the fermentation process. You knew fermentation had started when froth started to form on top and within days the frothing would become quite vigorous and might even overflow over the top. This was why it was important not to seal the container and leave it open. The mesh allowed for this and also stopped any animals getting inside. All the added grape skins would be floating on top with the froth and the bubbles. There was also a particular smell associated with this very aggressive chemical process of turning sugars into alcohol…. wine, *"vino"*, which I can smell clearly to this very day! I know it and can recognise it ANYWHERE! The smell of FERMENTATION!

After about seven days, the frothing had stopped, the grape skins had fallen to the bottom of the container, the wine was almost clear, quite drinkable and the process was complete. But the wine was too young *"troppo giovane"*, to drink straight away. It was now decanted from the containers, the sludge and the grape skins on the bottom and placed in receptacles, either wooden barrels or glass *"damiganni"*, which my father preferred and sealed for up to three months. This was the clarifying stage. In this stage the wine became crystal clear and separated from any particulates, which settle to the bottom as sludge due to gravity. These containers were stored in a cool location usually in a cellar or *"cantina"*. This was very important because if the wine became too hot, the fermentation process would start again in the containers and the wine would become *"Acetic Acid"*…. Vinegar…. Wine Vinegar!

After three months the wine was ready to drink and be decanted and transferred into four litre flagons (about fifty of them). He was very proud of his wine and drank it every day. I only drank it if I was desperate. I was desperate a lot! The bottles of tomatoes and flagons of wine were kept under the house because we didn't have a cellar and was the coolest place of the house. Access was very restricted as there was only about 80cm height above the ground so it was my job to crawl on all fours under the house. It was tight even for me, but I persevered. It wasn't too bad. We'd put pieces of cardboard on the ground so I didn't get soiled, as the ground was just bare earth as you'd expect under the floorboards of a house. In fact, under the house there was a level of tranquillity and serenity that I didn't get above the floorboards, which I enjoyed!

I don't know how it came about but in one particular year, my dad came out by stating that, women who were menstruating could not participate in the wine making process. Apparently, their involvement would turn the wine into vinegar! What a load of horse-shit I thought to myself. Another one of his *"crazy-arsed"* superstitious beliefs or myths that some old fart had told him. I thought to myself, this is bullshit, my mother has been making wine with us and she's a woman, I think?

Then one day I remembered that when I was very young, she had a hysterectomy!

1

2

3

4

5

Wine Making
1: Father,
2: Father,
3: Brother & Mother
4: Mother,
5: Father
   Photos circa 1991

Wine Making
1: Father, Nick, mother and niece Michelle 2: Nick and mother
3: Father, Nick, Michelle and mother
4: Father, Nick, & Michelle
5 & 6: Wine containers
   Photos circa 1990
7: My mother coming back from her hysterectomy operation,
8: Nick and mother
   Photos circa 1970

• Making Salami

Another important event in the yearly, *"Radice Famiglia"* culinary calendar was salami making. We're not talking one or two kilograms here! We're talking twenty or thirty kilograms. This was a big event, one which I didn't mind too much as, although it was a time-consuming process, it wasn't too laborious. This was done in the coldest months of the year, mid-July. Cold weather is an essential ingredient in the drying process. If it was too warm, the salami would not dry properly and could go off. The cold inhibited bacteria from growing inside the salami.

The meat had to be pork. Pork was important because of its fat content. The meat could not be lean. One of the most important factors to making good and tasty salami was the fat content. The meat had to be fatty otherwise it would be too tough and unable to be eaten. It would be like *"prosciutto"* or *"copa"* rather than salami. That's why butchers' have very soft hands, it's because of the fat (lard) which is in the meat and this moisturises their hands!

In the early years, we did everything ourselves, we minced the meat using a hand mincer, extra fat was added if needed, according to personal preference. Once the meat had been minced, it was placed in a big container. Now came the creative process, adding extra ingredients to personalise the salami. At this stage chilli, pepper, salt, paprika, fennel *"finocchio"* seeds all could be added to create your own particular salami, *"picante"* (hot) or *"dolce"* (sweet). No chemical additives or preservatives was added, everything was natural! A sample was fried and tasted to see if all the ingredients worked well. I like this part, especially with a slice of crusty *"pane di casse"*, *"molto delicioso"*. Sublime!

The next step was to fill the salami skins, which are actually pig intestines! This was originally done by hand, wrapping the skin around the end of an aluminium funnel and feeding the salami mince into it, which filled the salami skin, until there was one long salami at the end of the funnel. It was very important that there were no air pockets. The salami mince had to be packed in tight, for uniformity of drying. Then, every ten centimetres or so, it was twisted was to make five or six knobs of salami. These were hung up and using a needle, the skins were randomly punctured. This was to allow the fat to escape in the smoking and drying process.

Once all the salami had been made, they were hung in a smoke house. In our case it was the outside BBQ built by my father, the one with wonky sides which was converted by placing a sheet of corrugated iron as a roof and the salami was hung underneath. Every night a fire was lit but it was very important NOT to have flames, only smoke was wanted. This was very important as you did not want to cook the salami, only to dry it using smoke. The smoke also gave flavour to the salami. The fat from the salami would start to ooze out as it started to dry and it would drop on the charcoals which would produce more smoke and so the process went. This was carried out nightly for a week until the salami had shrunk and shrivelled in size quite noticeably. Now it was time to taste the salami. A nob was cut and sliced open, it should be a deep maroon colour, the slices were divvied out and placed once again on a piece of crusty "panne di case" and bitten into. No need for butter, the salami had taken care of all that. Heaven!

However, it didn't always work out, sometimes the weather changed and it was unseasonably warm, this is when my father would start to swear *"a va fan culo"*, *"putana"*, *"merda"*, *"porco miseria"*, were the most common ones. The most common issues were when the inside of the salami might have holes in it or it, might be a grey colour meaning it had gone off. In these cases, the only thing to do was to salvage as much of the salami as possible and throw the rest away. My father did this with gritted teeth and a knife in his heart.

He took these things very personally!

In fact, he took EVERYTHING, very personally!

Not everything was good homemade bottles of tomatoes, wine or salami and crusty *"pane di case"*, in the *"Radice Famiglia"* household!

Making Salami
1: Zia Donnatamaria, mother, nonna Radice, cousin Geraldine
Photo taken in Difesa, Italy 1979
3, 4, 5, 6: Salami and wine casks in the garage in Five Dock
7, 8: Homemade salami

The Great Salami Robbery

I'm not sure whether this story is just an urban myth, a tall tale or it actually happened but it was told to me by my uncle, Zio Francesco Russo with great relish and delight.

It happened on Christmas eve in 2004, when the good villagers of San Fele were all gathered around a great huge bonfire in the piazza, drinking, eating singing and dancing to celebrate the festivities of the season. Unbeknownst to the revellers, there was skulduggery afoot, for in the middle of the night, under the cloak of darkness, a large truck was traversing the countryside stopping at empty farmhouses, whose occupants were celebrating in the village.

Some say it was an "inside" job, for there seemed to be meticulous precision regarding this clandestine operation. They moved stealthily from farmhouse to farmhouse, salami barn to salami barn, stealing all of the villages' salami. Not one nob of salami was left.

By the time word had gone out and reached the celebrating villagers, pandemonium broke out. Each farmer raced off to protect their precious, delicious, newly made salami, copa and ham. But they were all too late. The deed had been done. The salami was gone.

There were rumours that it was being taken to the north "Alt Italia", Florence, Milan, Bologna, where they love salami from the south. There was no evidence to prove this, the robbers were never caught and the salami was never retrieved.

Whether this is true or not is irrelevant, for the South hate the North and the North exploits the South. That's how it's always been and will probably continue to be.

Nevertheless, it's a great story!

• Making "Copa"

"Copa" is another Italian cured cold meat, deliciously made from pork neck. The pork neck is the ideal meat for this because it is rolled into a long cylindrical shape and it has striations of fat running through it which make it perfect for curing, drying and then air dried which turns it into a hard large salami. It has to be sliced very thinly otherwise it is almost impossible to eat as it is very hard, almost like jerky.

Once again, just like any cold meat this is done in the winter months. The pork neck is encased into a very large intestine and the enclosed in a cotton meshing net. This is then cured in brine for 24 hours, making sure that the brine is poured over it every couple of hours.

Now it is covered with different herbs and spices according to individual and regional tastes.

Traditionally, salt and pepper are the most common ingredients but some, who like their *"Copa"* hot, will also smother it in chilli flacks. It is then hung up to dry in a cold, moisture free environment. Then it is smoked every evening for about a week or until the *"Copa'* has turned a beautiful red colour. It is very important that it is smoked only. You do not want the meat to be cooked, only dried.

Now, once dried it is ready to be eaten or stored, either just left to hang or some like to place it into jars of oil.

Enjoy!

"The Copa" hanging & being dried & smoked

• Curing Olives

Sicilian Olives

Have you ever tried *"Sicilian olives"*? They have the best taste in the world. Well, you ain't tried nothing until you've tasted *"Olives alla Basillicata"*! They are to die for!

Back in the old country *"Pot Ash"* was used to cure the olives. *"Pot Ash" (Potassium Hydroxide)*, as the name suggests was the ash from under the pots which was used to cook with.

You need large, green olives which are then cured in a solution of *"Caustic Soda"* instead of *"Pot Ash"*. Wood ash didn't work. The wood here was different. It was too strong and turned the olives into mush.

"Casustic Soda" is *"Sodium Hydroxide"*!

Yes, *"Sodium Hydroxide"*, for all you chemistry nerds. The dilution required is 20g of *"Caustic Soda"* per 1 kilogram of olives. Water should be added to completely submerge the olives into a container with a lid. The olives must always remain submerged in the solution, so it is customary to put a plate or towel to keep the olives from rising to the surface which if they do, can then react with oxygen in the air and go off. Stir every couple of hours and after a while you will see that the solution becomes very dark almost black. These are all the fats which make the green olive bitter to eat, which have now leached out into the solution.

The olives are kept in the solution for approximately 24 hours or until soft but it is very important that the olives are not too soft otherwise, they can become mush.

Once this is done, the olives are washed until all the brown colour is rinsed out.

Then the olives which should be a brilliant green colour are put into a jar filled with brine and placed and stored away in a cool, dark place, usually in a fridge.

Enjoy!

Dried Black Olives

Most people don't realise that black olives are just green olives that have not been picked when they are green but have been allowed to ripen on the tree.

The process is much easier than curing green olives. All that is required is to put the black olives into a container and add salt to immerse all the olives so that they are completely covered by the salt. Cover and store in a cool, dark place, usually in a cellar.

Allow the olives to cure for a week or so until they are completely shrivelled up. Now wash all the salt off put into jars with oil, seasoned with herbs and spices of your own choice.

Delicious!

Hot Dried Black Olives

Another delicious way of serving the dried block olives is to fry them quickly for a couple of minutes in oil with garlic and hot chili flakes (for those that like a little bit of spice).

Put hot olives into a bowl and serve.

Amazing!

Crushed Green Olives

The method for crushing the green olives used by my parents was quite bizarre but very ingenious. They placed the whole green olives into a hessian bag, tied it up and then placed it under the wheel of my father's Valiant and rolled over it, Hey presto! Instantly crushed green olives. The pips (seeds) were removed and the crushed green olives were place into jars filled with salt.

These were left to cure for a week or so. Then washed and placed into jars with oil once again seasoned with herbs and spices (usually garlic, oregano, pepper, hot chilli flakes) of your own choice.

Then eat!

Magnifico!

Molto deliciouso!

Chapter 11: Other Yummy "Wog" Treats

• Making Ragu

I was taught to make ragu by mother when I was 7 years young and this was purely for practical reasons. My parents both worked, my mother coming home at about 5:30pm and my father at about 6:30pm. So, coming home from primary school at 3:30pm gave me plenty of time to make the ragu before my parents got home.

This was my afternoon job, to make the ragu ready for the pasta to be cooked when my parents came home.

Making ragu is very easy, the ingredients are few and simple to prepare.

Step 1: Put extra virgin olive oil into a pot/pan heat and add a few cloves of garlic and 1 onion.

Step 2: Cook until golden brown but making sure not to burn them *(no one likes burnt garlic and onions throughout the ragu and besides it doesn't look good)*.

Step 3: Add a can of diced/pureed tomatoes *(homemade if possible)* and bring to the boil. Allow to cook for about 5 minutes.

Step 4: Add 2 tablespoons of tomato paste/concentrate *(homemade if possible)*, and then add a cup of water and stir the tomato paste into the sauce. Add salt, pepper and chilli flakes *(if you like it a bit hot)*. Allow to cook for about 5 minutes, stirring regularly. You do not want the sauce to burn!

This will destroy the flavour of your ragu!

Step 5: This is the creative part and depends on regional factors and/or even individual tastes. Some people add a teaspoon of sugar, others add half a cup of milk to the ragu. This is to counterbalance the acid from the tomatoes. I was taught not to add any of these.

Step 6: This is the most crucial step in the whole process but which is always rushed. Make sure to simmer the ragu for a good length of time. I recommend about 2 hours.

You cannot make a good ragu in 20 minutes. This not a ragu. This is just a slightly cooked tomato sauce.

You will know when the ragu has been cooked enough simply by looking at it. What you should see is a layer of oil floating on the surface of the ragu. This is the indicator that your ragu has cooked for long enough and is now ready to be served on any pasta of your choice.

Some people like to remove this layer of oil with a spoon. I do not!

Make sure to add parmesan cheese and eat with crusty pane di casa (to wipe the plate clean).

Perfetto!

- Making Lentil Soup

Vito's "World Famous" Lentil Soup
(La Famosa Zuppa di Lenticchie di Vito)

Well, you might've come to the conclusion that Vito is a useless sod.
Good for northing!
Well, you're wrong!
He is good for something.
His "World Famous" lentil soup.

Have you tried it?
You don't know what your taste buds have missed out on.
Fernanda LO♥ES it!
And she knows her lentil soups!
She knows the difference between red, green & brown lentils.
Yes, there are 3 varieties.
Possibly even more!
Here is the recipe.
Follow these steps precisely.
Do not alter any.
Do not be creative.

Step 1:
To a large pot add...
...extra virgin olive oil *(preferably Italian)*.
...one large brown onion.
...plenty of garlic.
Fry until golden brown.
Do not burn!

Step 2: *(optional)*
Add...
...a can of diced tomatoes *(preferably Italian)*.
Fry for approximately 5 minutes.
Stir occasionally.
Do not burn!

Step 3:
Add approximately 2 cups of water.
(vegetable or chicken stock can be used instead)
Bring to the boil.
Stir occasionally.
Do not burn!

Step 4: *(optional)*
Add...
...diced carrots.
...diced potatoes.
Bring to the boil.
Stir occasionally.
Do not burn!

Step 5:
Lower temperature.
Let simmer for approximately 1 hour.
Stir occasionally.
If liquid is low, add water as required.
Do not burn!

Let cool.
Serve in a bowl with grated parmesan cheese sprinkled on top.

Enjoy!

Buon appetito!

"The Don"
03.12.2021

1, 2: Chocolate calzone
3: Biscotti
4: Canoli

1: Scarpadgue frizzelli
2: Pannetone

- **Porco, Maiale**
  (The slaughtering of a pig)

The killing, the slaughtering of an animal, any animal is a brutal, savage, barbaric and prehistoric act. In this case it was the slaughtering of a pig. The pig did not want to die. It took 8 big men to hold it down. It struggled and fought for its life, until it's very last breath. It was truly a horrifying experience. One which I would not want to experience ever again. I was asked to participate. I had no choice, really. My job was …
… to hold its tail. A very ignoble act in the eyes of the other men. A position of ridicule because I was the "Americano"!

I know we have to eat but there must be a better way than this to get our food!

I think I'll become a vegetarian!

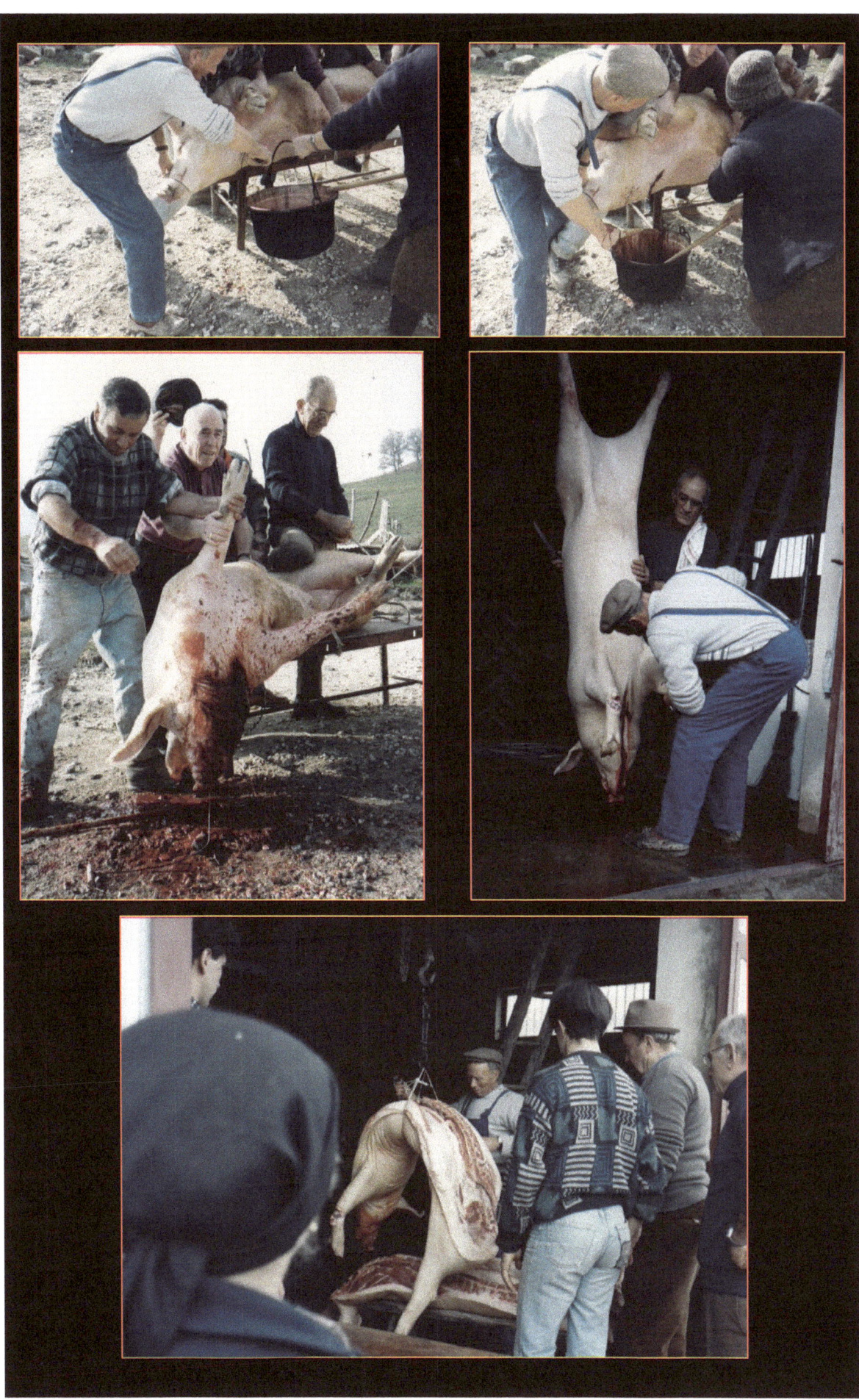

The slaughtering of a pig

Page 78 & 79:
1-6: the killing process
7: the carcass being cut up into pieces

This page:
8 & 9: My nonna (who was 96 years old) & my uncle (Zio Tonino) holding cut up pieces of the pig ready to be cooked

Chapter 12: The Golden Chariot

The greatest love of my father's life was his beloved and cherished *"Golden Chariot"*, his white *"Chrysler Valiant"*. He bought it in December 1969. It had a *"Hemi 245Hp V6 engine"* complete with a red chilli and the Devils horns fingers hanging from the rear-view mirror to the white rug on the rear window with the bobbing tiger's head, registration number, ADQ498! It was built like a tank. All steel. You could drive head on into a brick wall and the brick wall would come out of it second best. That's how strong it was! It was a beast! Fast, boy was it fast.! It would leave all other cars for dead! It was a petrol guzzler though, as were all cars of that era. No saving the environment of the planet in those days.

He still did not know how to drive when he bought it and he learnt on it. The only thing he had driven before was horse or his donkey. In fact, when he was driving, he drove like he was still riding his donkey. He would heave backwards and forwards in his seat, as if to urge the car to go faster.

Being a passenger when he drove, was not a pleasant or enjoyable experience. I never felt very comfortable because he was quite an erratic and impulsive driver at the best of times. He would love to give a bit of a work out every now and then when we would go out for a drive on a Sunday and take the freeway (yes, roads were actually *FREE* in those days), probably to go to farm to buy live chickens! He would love to accelerate to eighty or ninety miles per hour, it still had the Imperial Units on its speedometer, so he never was quite sure how many kilometres per hour he was actually go! He was the happiest on these occasions saying proudly, *"Abbiamo gettare?"*, *"are we going to throw it?"*. I would sit in the back which didn't have seat belts fitted and it wasn't compulsory to wear them, so I would lay flat on my back and watch the sky and the clouds wiz past as my father let the beast from its chains. He was flying! Sometimes he would fly and sing. This was when he was really happy!

My mother would tell him that he loved that car more than her. Which was absolutely true! He loved that car. Treated it like a queen. He kept it in pristine condition and whenever something was wrong with it, he never once balked at spending the money to fix it. He only used genuine *"Chrysler"* parts on it. Only the best would do for his *"Golden Chariot"* and he spent a lot of money on it over the thirty-three years that he had it.

I was with him on that terrible day when he was no longer able to renew his driver's license and could therefore no longer legally drive his beloved *"Golden Chariot"*. It was late January 2005, he was eighty-one years old and in NSW it is a requirement to have an eyesight test every year when a person becomes eighty. His eyesight had been deteriorating rapidly but as is common, he bluffed and fudged his way through. We went together to the *Five Dock Motor Registry*, he drove. I could see that he was nervous. I reassured him that everything would be fine. I was hoping for a miracle. We took a ticket and waited for his name to be called. We walked up to the counter and he was asked to read out the letters on the screen projected on the back wall. Straight away he said *"D A F G K"*. I was impressed. The person behind the counter asked him, *"Mr Radice, can you see the letters on the back wall?"*,

"Yes!", he replied. *"Can you please read them out for me?"* *"D A F G K"*, he replied. She turned to me a said *"Does your father understand?"* *"Yes"*, I replied. It's then I realised what he was doing, he had memorised letters from somewhere else and thought he could get away with it. He started to panic and tremble. *"Aiutami"*, "help me" he said to me. *"Non posso, papa!"*, *"I can't dad!"*. He started to cry. I drove his beloved *"Golden Chariot"* back home to Elizabeth Street. Old age is a *"Shithole"*!

He did drive it again a few times, illegally, mainly to *"All Hallows Church"* for Saturday evening mass. He sold it a neighbour a couple of months later and he cried again.

1: My father (seated inside "The White Chariot"), my mother & me in front of the Five Dock house
Circa 1970

2: Father, mother and Nick
Circa 1970

1: Nick, me, Zia Laura, mother & father
2: Me, my mother & father

All photos circa 1970

Chapter 13: In Search of the Meaning in Life

What are we here for? What is the purpose of our lives? Is there a meaning or is it all meaningless? A JOKE?

You are born, you struggle and then you die! Without a choice in any of these events! Struggling, that thing called LIVING, in between being born and dying, is like finding yourself in a rip. All you can do is try to negotiate it as best you can! There is no one to help you!

There is no map.

You are given no skills or techniques to help you.

You are far from land, there are no life guards to signal for help.

There is no point screaming or crying, there is no driftwood to grab on to, to cling on to.

You are all ALONE!

Is our existence just a farce?

Is this a comedy, a musical or a tragedy that we're living in!

Was GOD the answer? And if it was, which GOD? Whose GOD? There were too many Gods! Which one is the RIGHT GOD?

I was raised as a Roman Catholic, so I knew (more or less) about the Christian God but I was NEVER satisfied that it had all the answers for me. I look at people around me who believed in this God and found them to be hypocrites, say one thing and do something completely opposite. My parents for example, especially my father just used God for his own convenience. When things weren't working out for him. He even abused his God, swore at him but then prayed for his help. I was always amazed at his duality, how on one hand he prayed to his God for help but when things were going pear shaped and his prays weren't being answered, or so he thought, he would turn on him. Blame God for looking after him!

These questions vexed and perplexed me.

I went to Drummoyne Boys' High School and there I formed friendships that have lasted to this very day. Almost fifty years later!

These guys are my REAL brothers! My REAL family!

Blood means SHIT!

I was a sensitive teenager! My closest friends from school were also very sensitive. We were not like the other boys at my school. They were into fast, hotted up cars, disco, getting dressed up and looking shmick!

We were intellectuals! Listened to different music: Bob Dylan, Leonard Cohen, Neil Young, Joni Mitchell, Jethro Tull, Led Zeppelin, Pink Floyd and others.

We didn't like cars like the other boys.
We played music.
We wrote stories.
We wrote poetry.
We were artistic.
We valued art.
We took **DRUGS**!

We philosophised.
We went to see plays.
We went to music concerts.
We got drunk.
Some of us had girlfriends.
Some of us had sex.
But not ME!
We got STONED!
We dropped ACID (LSD)!

We were interested in Eastern Philosophies & mystic writing & mysticism in general.
We were interested in Esoteric Writings.
We were interested in Psychology.
We were interested in Religions & Religious Beliefs.
We were interested in Spirituality.
We were interested in Spiritual Enlightenment
We were interested in High Levels of Consciousness.
We were interested in Death & beyond! Is there anything after *Death* or is this *ALL* there is?
We were interested, enquired, studied & sought the *Meaning of Life*!

I was particularly interested in and fascinated in:
The Religious Feeling,
Religiosity,
Altered States,
Psychotherapy,
Cosmology,
Astrology,
Supernatural Phenomena,
Extra-terrestrial Beings,
Surrealism, especially Dali.

Books and authors that inspired me and influenced my way of thinking and that are still an intrinsic part of my very fabric today (for a variety of reasons) were:

- Buddha
- Hermann Hesse
- Franz Kafka
- Samuel Coleridge

- Homer
- The Mahabharata
- The Epic of Gilgamesh
- Timothy Leary
- The Tibetan Book of the Dead
- George Gurdjieff
- Gabriel Gibran
- Carlos Castaneda
- Krishnamurti
- Niccolò Machiavelli
- Albert Camus
- Jack Kerouac
- Bertrand Russell
- Fydor Dostovesky
- Aleksandr Solzhenitsyn
- Carl Jung
- Sigmund Freud
- Jean-Paul Sartre
- Isabelle Allende
- Eric Von Daniken
- Petrarch
- Mahatma Ghandi
- Zen and The Art of Motorcycle Maintenance by Robert M. Pirsig
- Mario Rodriguez Cobos *(Silo)*

1: 1975 2: 1979 3: 1980 4: 1983

My favourite albums (this page),
My favourite films (next page)

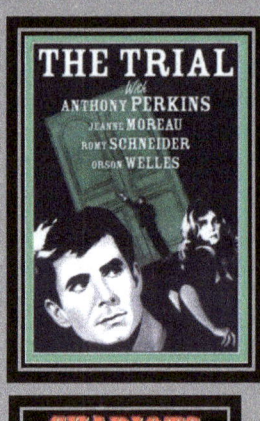
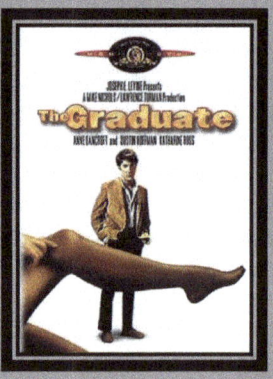

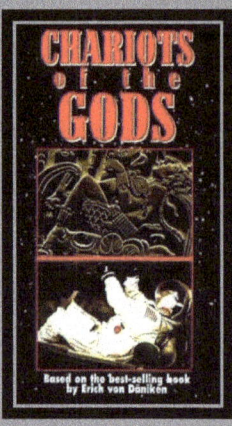

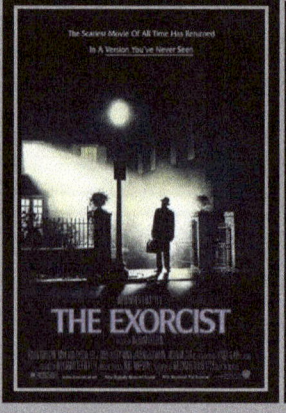
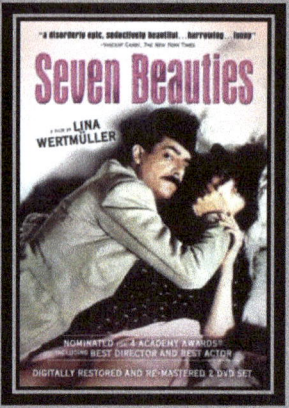

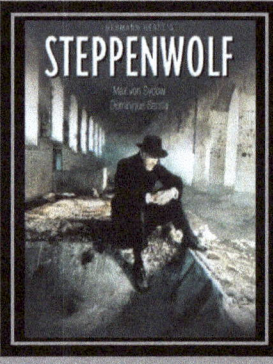

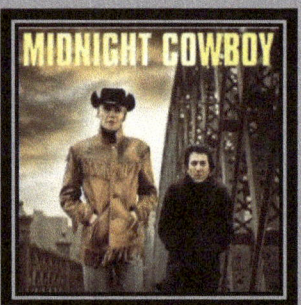
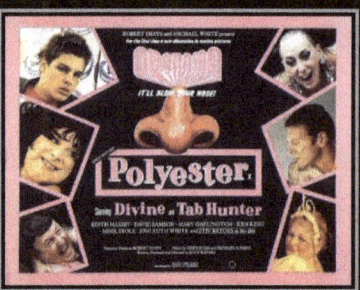

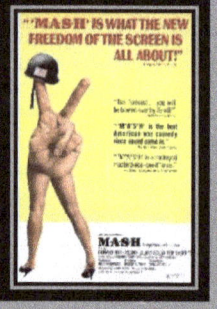

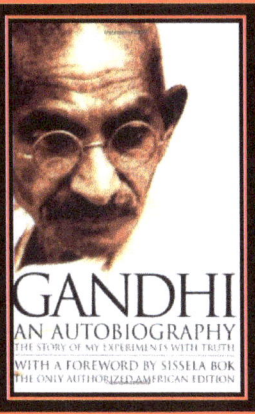

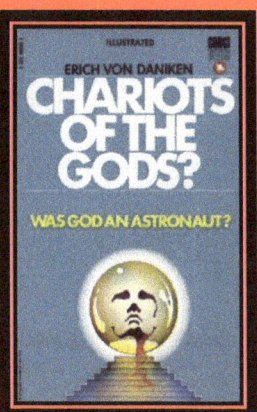
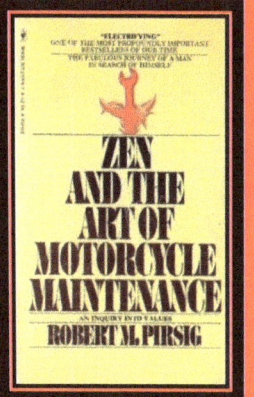

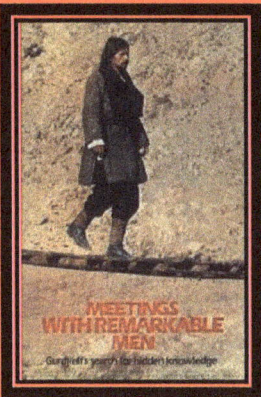

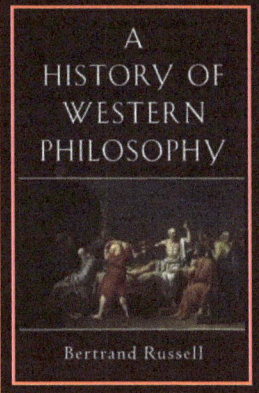
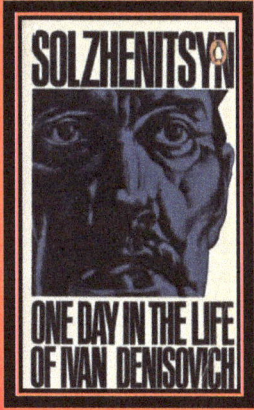

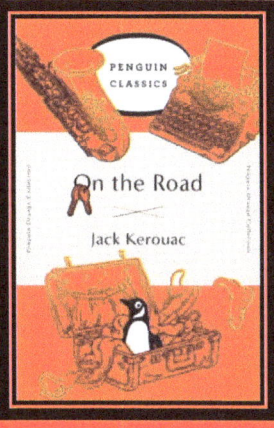

Chapter 14: Living in the 1970s & 80s

Greg & I
Circa 1978-79

The 1970's were times of great social and political upheaval as Australia, a young nation, an island, no other countries with which to share a land border, a very small population, and an enormous land mass, trying to establish its identity and place within the community of global nations.

Gough Whitlam and the *"Australian Labor Party"* were elected into power and government on 5th December 1972.

Whitlam was elected as PM, with his deputy PM, Lance Barnard, they formed a two-man cabinet and passed a raft of new legislation in the first few days.

They were called *"The Dynamic Duo"*!

They were very well prepared!

New laws passed included:
- *The abolition of conscription* (which up until this stage was compulsory for all males who turned eighteen. They could be drafted and sent to fight in Vietnam, a war in which Australia was involved by supporting the USA).

  My brother, Nick, coincidently had received his draft papers, (he was one of the unlucky chaps chosen out of a ballot to be sent off to fight in Vietnam. He was supposed to leave in February, 1973).

  How lucky was he and many others in the same situation!

- *The legislation to make ALL education FREE*, including tertiary!
- The establishment of *"Medibank"*: free, universal health and medical care for EVERYONE!
- Legislated for *Equal Rights and Pay for women*.
- Recognised *"First Nation's Peoples"* as the original custodians of the nation.

On the 11th November 1975 the greatest upheaval in Australian politics took place: The *Whitlam Labor Government* was dismissed by the *Governor General at the time Sir John Kerr*!

This was an event so massive the like of which Australia have never experienced before or since!
It was so big it rocked the very foundations of our democratic system!

It was the equivalent to a political "nuclear bomb" being dropped onto the Australian political landscape!

It changed EVERYTHING!

The Dismissal of the Whitlam government in 1975 started my interest in politics!

I thought the Dismissal by the Queen to be interference into our sovereignty and to be totally unconstitutional!

The Dismissal had a profound effect on me and my political ideas!

How could a democratically elected government by so trivially and casually dismissed!

What happened to the "Will of the People"?

"The mandate" to government given to it by the people?

The fact that an unelected opposition party (The Liberal Party) was put into power without being elected!

I was shocked and flabbergasted at these events!

I still cannot reconcile these events today, fifty years later!

Since then, Whitlam has become a political cult figure, both revered by "The Left" for his radical reforms, loathed and despised by "The Right' for his very radical & reckless, political agenda! Most criticised his government for (supposedly) mismanagement of the economy, which I do not agree with.

People either loved or hated him!

I loved him!

I loved his intellect, his araldite wit, humour, his love of culture and his love of the ordinary person.

He was a visionary!

An independent Australia free from the shackles of imperialist rule and foreign multinational and Nations!

He gave Australia a new sense of identity, self-worth and belief in itself that it did not have before!

He gave Australia a sense of maturity, a strength to be able to stand on its own on the world stage and not just an appendage of Great Britain!

We even got a new Anthem *"Advance Australia Fair!"*, although a lot thought *"Waltzing Matilda"* captured more of the Australian larrikin spirit!

Whitlam and his government were dismissed at 4:45pm on the 11th November 1975 by The Governor General, the Queen's Representative in Australia (unelected), by a decree from Queen Elizabeth II, the unelected monarch of Australia (most people don't know that Australia is a *"Constitutional Monarchy and NOT a "Republic")!* These words have been cemented into Australia's history:

"Well may we say "God save the Queen", because nothing will save the Governor-General! The Proclamation which you have just heard read by the Governor-General's Official Secretary was countersigned Malcolm Fraser, who will undoubtedly go down in Australian history from Remembrance Day 1975 as Kerr's <u>cur</u>. They won't silence the outskirts of Parliament House, even if the inside has been silenced for a few weeks ... Maintain your rage and enthusiasm for the campaign for the election now to be held and until polling day".

-**Gough Whitlam's statement upon his dismal as Prime Minister of Australia**
https://en.wikipedia.org/wiki/1975_Australian_constitutional_crisis

Gough Whitlam, Prime Minister (left), Lance Barnard, Deputy Prime Minister and Gough Witlam, 1972

Paul Keating (treasurer) and Bob Hawke (Prime Minister), 1983

Gough Whitlam, Prime Minister (right), Sir John Kerr, Governor General (bottom), 1975

Malcolm Fraser, Liberal Party (conservatives) won the subsequent federal election and a period of austerity followed with lots of funding cuts justified on the previous *"Labor Government's"* mismanagement of the economy and its inability to reign in foreign debt.

"The Labor Party" (Democratic Socialist) was re-elected to government under the leadership of Bob Hawke. Hawke was a populist leader with enormous charisma but a big disappointment!

He had a unionist background being a former leader of the *"ACTU" (Australian Council of Trade Unions)*, the overarching body overseeing all the trade unions in Australia. In this role, he become known as *"The Great Communicator"* for being able to bring warring parties to conference table and negotiating deals, accords and solutions amicably, in which both parties walked away happy!

However, he was the one who introduced the HECS (Higher Education Contribution Scheme).

I love the use of the word "contribution"!

Tertiary education was No longer FREE!

The thin edge of the edge was introduced and it has gotten worse ever since!

Although he did reintroduce in "Medicare", universal medical care for all which is still the backbone of the health system throughout Australia now!

In my late teens, I went to university and started hanging around the inner city, especially Glebe and Newtown. A place that I have extremely fond memories of was *"The Valhalla Cinema"* in Glebe, which has now been converted into apartments. The façade is still there though and when I walk past it now, I get very sad that it is no longer there for others to experience the joy and happiness that I enjoyed.

In the 1980s, it showed 'Art House' films not shown anywhere else. It also had midnight screenings. Many a time was spent with my friends, *"stoned out of our heads"* watching Fellini, John Waters or Andy Warhol films.

Movies that I was inspired by included:

- *"The Tin Drum"* (by *Gunter Grass* an amazing movie and an even more amazing book.)
- *"The Tree of Wooden Clogs"*
- *"Midnight Cowboy"*
- *"Le Grande Bouffe"*
- *"Steppenwolf"*
- *"The Exorcist"*
- *"Star Wars"* (especially the idea of "The Force")
- *"Chariots of the Gods?"* (based on the book by Erik Von Daniken)
- *Koyaanisqatsi* (from the Hopi word meaning *"life out of balance"*)
- *Powaqqatsi*
- *Mondo Cane*

- *A Clockwork Orange*
- *2001: A Space Odyssey*
- *Planet of the Apes*
- *The Bicycle Thief* (Vittorio da Sica; Italian "Neo-Realism" cinema)
- *The Godfather*
- *The Exorcist*
- *Erasurehead*

Albums/songs that I was inspired by included:

- *Blood on the Tracks (Bob Dylan)*
- *Desire (Bob Dylan)*
- *Dirge (Bob Dylan)*
- *Recent Songs (Leonard Cohen)*
- *Songs from the Woods (Jethro Tull)*
- *Aqualung (Jethro Tull)*
- *Thick as a Brick (Jethro Tull)*
- *The Minstrel in the Gallery (Jethro Tull)*
- *Too Old to Rock'n'Roll (But Too Young to Die) (Jethro Tull)*
- *Dark Side of the Moon (Pink Floyd)*
- *Wish You Were Here (Pink Floyd)*
- *The Wall (Pink Floyd)*
- *Led Zeppelin IV (Led Zeppelin)*
- *Dire Straits (Dire Straits)*
- *O Caritas (Cat Stevens)*
- *Age of Aquarius (The 5th Dimension)*

Places that I liked to hang out at included *(though most, sadly, no longer exist)*:

- *The Valhalla*, Glebe
- *The Roxy*, Darlinghurst
- *La Vina*, Leichhardt
- *The Bayview Tavern*, Birkenhead Point, Drummoyne
- *The Pickled Parrot*, Gladesville
- *The Three Weeds (Rose, Shamrock & Thistle)*, Rozelle
- *Haberfield Rowing Club*
- Drummoyne Rowing Club
- Badde Manors, Glebe

Who could have ever foreseen where all these interests would have led me to and what the future had in store for me and my friends!

Drummoyne Boys' High School motto:
"Vincit Qui Se Vincit"
"He Conquers Who Conquers Himself"

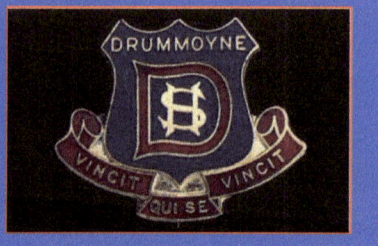

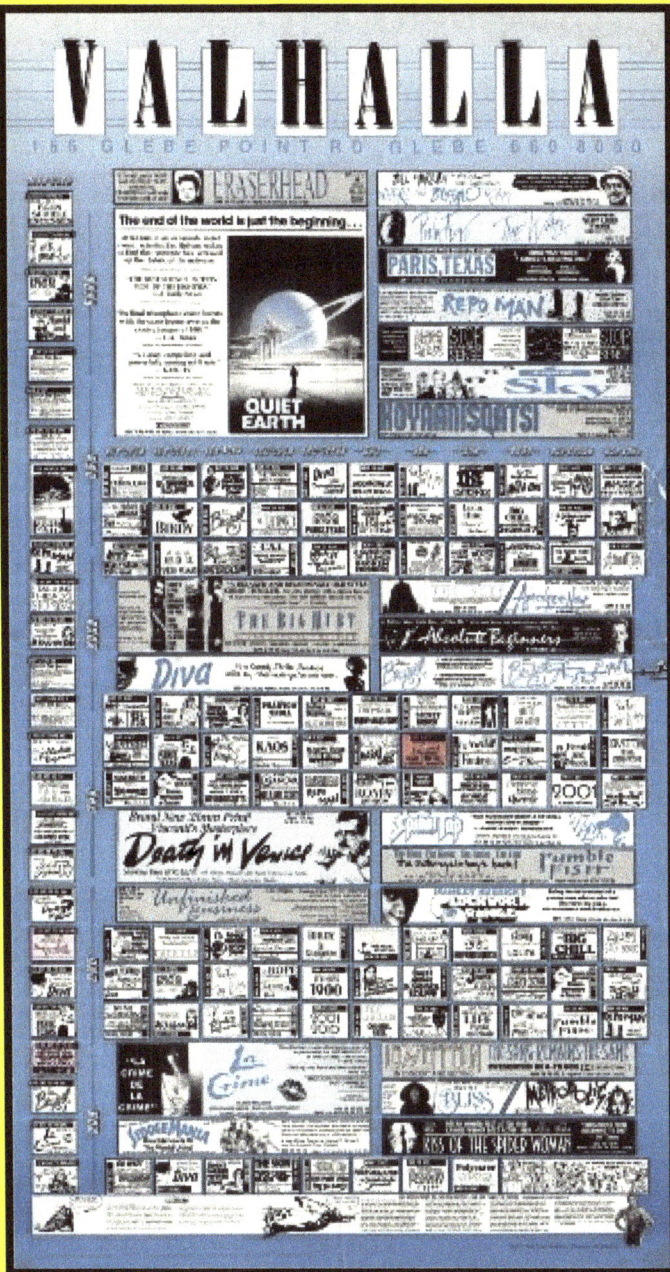

The Valhalla Cinema in Glebe

Chapter 15: My Life in a CULT

I have always been interested and searched for *"The Meaning of Life"* and so may come as no surprise that on particular day my friend Greg introduced me to ***"The Community for Human Development"***.

We had both taken the day off from I from *"Kenso Kindy"*, *NSW University* and Greg from *Sydney University*.

We were in my bedroom *"chewing the fat"*, discussing existential ideas *(basically wanking on, as seemingly so called, pseudo intellectual teenage boys do)*, when he says that he had had an amazing experience and if I was interested to experience it as well. He said that he had done a *"Guided Experience"* carried out by another mutual school friend ours Phil.

All I had to do was lay back on my bed, close my eyes, relax and follow the story that the narrated. (Greg had an amazing memory).

His memory abilities were astonishing!

He could remember every word and verse of many very long *Bob Dylan*, *Leonard Cohen* and *Arlo Guthrie* songs such as;
- *"Mr Tambourine Man"*,
- *"Idiot Wind"*,
- *"Tangled Up in Blue"*,
- *"Stuck Inside a Mobile with the Memphis Blues Again"*,
- *"The Ballad of Frankie Lee & Judas Priest"*,
- *"Lily, Rosemary & the Jack of Hearts"*,
- *"Suzanne"*,
- *"Famous Blue Raincoat"*,
- *"Chelsea Hotel"*,
- *"So Long, Marianne"*,
- *"Alice's Restaurant"*,
- *"The Motorcycle Song"* and so many others.

So, it was no surprise that he could remember it word for word, in its entirety!

It was called ***"The Journey"***!

It BLEW my mind!

I had NEVER had such a MIND-BLOWING experience before!

Greg asked if I had liked it?

"It was like having a trip!", I said.

He said that there was a group that did this stuff and they called it doing *"Internal Work"* and this, was called a *"Guided Experience"*. The next meeting was on Friday night, 7:30pm at Kirribilli Neighbourhood Centre, if I was interested in going along. I said sure, why not?

So off, I went on that Friday night.

Kirribilli Neighbourhood Centre is a very impressive Victorian mansion with a bullnose, wrap-around verandah, set amidst a beautiful garden, overlooking The Sydney Opera House and The Sydney Harbour Bridge. You couldn't get a more picturesque or beautiful setting even if you could imagine it!

It was raining!

I LOVE rain! Especially rainy nights!

The room was at the front of the building, the first door to your left as you entered the corridor facing a staircase which led to the upstairs floor. I entered the room. It was a large room with its walls and ceiling painted white and a bay window facing the street. A group of about twenty people were sitting in a circle in the middle of the room. I sat on a chair.

It was explained by a person (all in white), running the meeting that we were going to do some *"Internal Work"*, which would include a *"relaxation"*, a *"Guided Experience"*, called *"Death"* and afterwards *"discussion of our experiences"*. He asked everyone to close our eyes and follow what he was reading.

It was a totally new experience for me. I really enjoyed it! It felt light and euphoric.

After the meeting my friends and I remained talking and we were invited to continue our discussions at his place, which was an apartment just down the road. So, we all walked out into the rainy, windy night following him to his apartment.

There was something surreal and mystical that night!

A raining, windy night and the street lights and the dark, the shadows, the reflections, the glare, with you best friends, the view of the Sydney Opera House in front, going off to a complete stranger's apartment.

It was an ***ADVENTURE!***

The building was an old, brown brick "Art Deco" place and he lived in a one bed room apartment on the top floor. It had little furniture and so we all sat on the carpeted floor.

We talked for what seemed an eternity. Finally, we decided to leave at about 11:00pm.

It was still raining!

I was HOOKED!

The person's name was ***Nestor Valenzuela***.

The group was called ***"The Community for Human Development"***!

Chapter 16: The Community for Human Development

Nestor was in his late twenties, short, quite charismatic, always wore white or beige clothes, from Santiago, Chile and had brought *"The Community"* with him to Sydney, Australia in about 1978. He had become involved in Chile, a couple of years earlier. He started running meetings all around Sydney, usually hiring rooms in Neighbourhood centres. Phillip saw a poster on a wall at Sydney University where he was attending. The poster simply stated, *"In Search of the Meaning in Life"*, this caught Phil's attention and he decided to attend the lunchtime meeting.

This is how my group of friends become involved.

Most of my friends became involved, to a greater or lesser degree.

In the early days, the meetings involved carrying out *"Internal Work"*, doing "Guided Experiences", which Nestor had photocopies *(it was not until 1980 that a book called, "The Book of Community" was published)* and later after the meetings go back to his place where we would continue the discussions and Nestor would tell us more about *"The Community"* and stories of *Cobos*.

"Power, sex or money" are the three motivating reasons a person does something, *Nestor* used to often say.

Nestor explained that there was a *"Structure"* and a mechanism called *"Lines"* and that we were connected through him to *"Tito's Line"*, who lived in Tokyo, Japan.

Apparently, in the early days when *"The Community"* was being formed, *Cobos*, the founder had formed a team of people with whom he took away from society into the mountains of Argentina, where they carried out intense "Internal Work". They were asked to leave their families, friends, jobs, studies and devout themselves to the studies of *"Self-Awareness"*. This they did for a couple years. When *Cobos* thought they were ready, these people were sent on *"Missions"* to different parts of the globe to build *"The Community"*.
The places that they were sent to, that I know of were, Japan, USA, Sri Lanka, Canada, Iceland and Spain.

Nestor was NOT a part of this team and he was not sent here on a mission nor was he ever a part of *Cobos*' inner circle.

In those early days all we did was "Internal Work", which we loved. In weekly meetings and weekend retreats, more intensive work from a book called *"Self-Liberation"* written by *Luis A. Amman* was carried out.

I loved this!

One my favourite places where we would go for a weekend retreat was called *"Ahmisa"* *("hut-happy-omen")* in Cheltenham *(I wonder if it is still available today? I guess I'll have to "Google" it!)*. It was an open, one room hut, in a bushland setting, hired from *"NSW Parks and Wildlife"*, available for non-profit organisations to use.

Other places we used were:

- Woodstock Neighbourhood Centre, Burwood
- Annandale Neighbourhood Centre, Annandale
- Surry Hills Neighbourhood Centre, Surry Hills
- Summer Hill Community Centre, Summer Hill
- Bondi Beach Community Centre, Bondi Beach
- Drummoyne Community Centre, Drummoyne
- A member's holiday cottage, high on a cliff, overlooking the beach at Queenscliff
- Newtown Neighbourhood Centre, Newtown Locale
- Rozelle Neighbourhood Centre, Rozelle
- Gladesville Neighbourhood Centre, Gladesville
- Chatswood Neighbourhood Centre, Chatswood
- Lavender Bay Neighbourhood Centre, North Sydney
- Bankstown Community Centre, Bankstown
- Kings Cross, Locale
- Stanmore, Locale

One very important person who arrived from Germany in 1980 is *Angelika*. I was attracted and mesmerised by her as soon as I saw her. She was like an *"Amazonian Warrior"*. Strong, opinionated, fearless and very sexy!

She shared a house in Balmain at this time with another member called *Nicola*, who had just arrived from Italy. Later on, that year she would marry *Nestor* and the moved into a place on King Street, Newtown which had a shop front and this was used as a *"Locale"* (meeting place). They lived upstairs and the *"Locale"* was used for meetings.

It was a fantastic place!

One of most treasured memories and unforgettable experiences was a one-week retreat that I went to in *Sri Lanka* 1981 with another member called *Daniel*. There were about fourteen other members from and run by a guy called *Julian*. It took place in a very remote part at a place called *"World's End"*!

This was an amazing location. It was a very remote inaccessible place, high in the mountains and to get there we had to travel along a very steep, windy, narrow dirty road. The road was treacherous and perilous. It was not wide enough for two cars, let alone big trucks and many times we almost on the very edge of the road. Below us was a steep ravine. A fall from here would have certainly meant a lot of injuries, if not death. It was very scary but also very exciting. We went there in a mini bus, all the members travelling together and it took a couple of hours to get to the summit.

Once there we were greeted by amazing views of the mountains and the valley below, that stretched out forever before us. We were literally *"above the clouds"*.

It is 1,067 metres above sea level with a 300 metre vertical drop.

The place was an old colonial estate house complete with outhouses and other nooks and crannies. It is only about 500 metres, a short walk away, through a forest, which took about fifteen minutes by foot! Locals told us that there were tigers and snakes in there but I didn't encounter any. Maybe they were just jungle myths to excite and scare the tourists!

This was really *"Heaven"*!

It is now a guest house called *"Hatale Mini World's End Bungalow"*.

I could not tell my parents I was going off to Sri Lanka for ten days, so I told them I was going to *Surfers' Paradise, Queensland* with some friends instead.

Another memorable weekend retreat was held in a beach house in Kilcare, Central Coast. We arrived late on a Friday night driving up from Sydney. It was cold, raining and windy, a perfect scenario for *"Internal Work"*!

You know how I love this sort of weather!

It was right on the beach.

An awesome place!

Other retreats were held at Lane Cove River Park, Lane Cove, in the convention centre. A bushland setting in the heart of suburbia!
A weeklong retreat was held in Como, high in the mountain country. It was summer time (early January) and very hot during the day but very cold at night. It was a sprawling chalet (probably designed for the snow season), it had a huge open fireplace around which you could sit. It was fantastic!
These were my favourite times!

From top L-R, Locale on Kings St., Newtown, Symbols, retreat at Lane Cove

From top L-R, Vito, Vito, Greg and Tree at Surry Hills Neighbourhood Centre, 21st September,

From top L-R, Vito, Vito, Nestor, Vito, at a rally, (Centre) at a march, (Bottom 4) Ahimsa

Previous page: In Singapore & Colombo, Sri Lanka
This page: Retreat at World's End, Sri Lanka, 1981

A group photo of all who participated in the retreat.
Daniel and I are at the front left. Sherwin is second from the right

The building of friendships, sharing experiences, discussing ideas, forming new relationships, reconnecting with old friendships, eating, singing and learning together!

A real community of fellow human beings together on the same adventure, same journey!

We ran Community meetings in Bondi Beach in the *"Craft Room"* of the Bondi Beach Pavilion.
What a location!

The *"Craft Room"* was a long narrow room, on the inside of the Pavilion. The Pavilion had an open, outdoor theatre, in the middle of it. It was an open quadrangle.
We were chronic smokers and on one particular night we smoked so many cigarettes that the room became completely full of smoke. One new person, after the meeting said that she really loved the ideas but would not be returning because we smoked too much!

I thought it was mandatory to smoke, if one was to be an intellectual and a revolutionary!

It was on a cold and wintery, Wednesday night, after a *"Community"* meeting, in Bondi. Phil, Greg and I decided to go to *"The Cross"* (Kings Cross), the notorious red-light district of Sydney. It has now become gentrified but back in my day it was it was sleazy and notorious. Some would say that it was bad and needed to change!

I, on the other hand, loved it. Loved its personality, its characters, its venues and the night life, which now has ALL gone.

Kings Cross is no longer the *Kings Cross* of my youth, in the 1980s and 90s. Now, it has become gentrified and acceptable.

With the enormous urban development going on and the introduction of the *"lock-out"* laws, Sydney has lost its vibrancy, culture, venues, it's LIFE!

One of my favourite places where I used to be a regular in *"The Cross"* was the *"Manzil Room"*, (it was located at 15 Springfield Avenue and operated until 1990, when the venue changed its name to *"Springfields"*). It no longer exists, like so many places. But it still lives on in my memory. This place was not a place for *"lock-out"* laws. It didn't open its doors until 11:00pm. It had live bands playing but they didn't get on stage till 1:00am or 2:00am. So, this was not a place for an early night, more like an early morning! Say 6am or 7am in the morning.

Here we were outside a brothel to pick up a prostitute!

We walked into a brothel and all the girls we sitting watching TV. We didn't know what was going on. They all seemed to be very excited at what was happening. We asked them what was going on and one of the girls told us it was the wedding of the century!

Prince Charles was marrying Lady Diana Spencer!
I couldn't believe it!

Here we were going to get a screw on the night of this momentous, world-wide event!

It seemed serendipitous!

We each chose a girl, although they seemed reluctant to leave the ceremony!
I was led through a corridor, up some stairs, into a very small dark room, no bigger than a shoebox.

She said it was $40 for a fuck and $20 for a blowjob. I said I'll have a fuck please and gave her the money. She fell on the bed, still with her clothes on and said, *"Come on get it in!"*.

I knew at this point that this was not going to go well.
I got on top of her, both still clothed, and I pulled my dick out of my pants.
She lay beneath me completely motionless. Which was very off putting. I tried to get an erection but try as I might, I could not.

After a while she said, "Is it in yet?".

By this stage I knew I had FAILED!

I got off her, zipped up my pants and said I was done and walked out.

I was not a pleasurable or pleasant experience!

Afterwards, outside back on the wintery streets of Kings Cross when the others asked me how it was, I said it was FANTASTIC!
How could I tell them the truth?

Later on, I realised she was as high as a kite. Poor thing didn't have a clue what was going on!

This was my first sexual experience 29th July, 1981.

I was twenty-two years old!

I went outside and waited for the others to finish. Phil came out first and little while later Greg came out asking Phil if he could borrow another $20 for a "blowjob". He hadn't finished yet. Phil begrudgingly gave him another $20.

A good night was had by all!

Kings Cross in the 1970s & 80s

In 1983, it all came to a head for *Nestor*.

A guy called *Antonio* moved to Sydney, Australia in November 1984.

Antonio was Argentinian from Buenos Aires. He was tall and held himself with an air of authority. He was always impeccably dressed and had a casual elegance about him. He claimed that was because of his father's background, being a military man and he himself having been sent to a military school.
I was impressed by him straight away! He seemed very cultured to me!

I liked his style!

In fact, I copied it!

Within a month *Nestor* had imploded and left!

A new chapter had begun!

I saw *Nestor* a few more times, once, late on a Saturday night in Kings Cross, Sydney. He was surrounded by group of girls, sitting in front of a bank. He was still wearing white clothes, although somewhat dishevelled and looking quite "out of it"!

I think he had become a "guru"!

The last time I saw him was in Florence, Italy at the *"First Congress of The International Humanist Party"*. He looked fantastic and seemed to be in good spirits.

A couple of years later I heard that he had been killed in road accident in Santiago, Chile!

I was shocked!

I couldn't believe it!

I was very sad!

I cried!

Tears welled up in my eyes! They rolled down my cheeks, down over my lips down my chin.

I felt that something had been torn from inside me, that I had lost a part of me.

It affected my greatly and I was surprised by that!

I had not really thought that much about him, if at all.
Funny how things affect you!

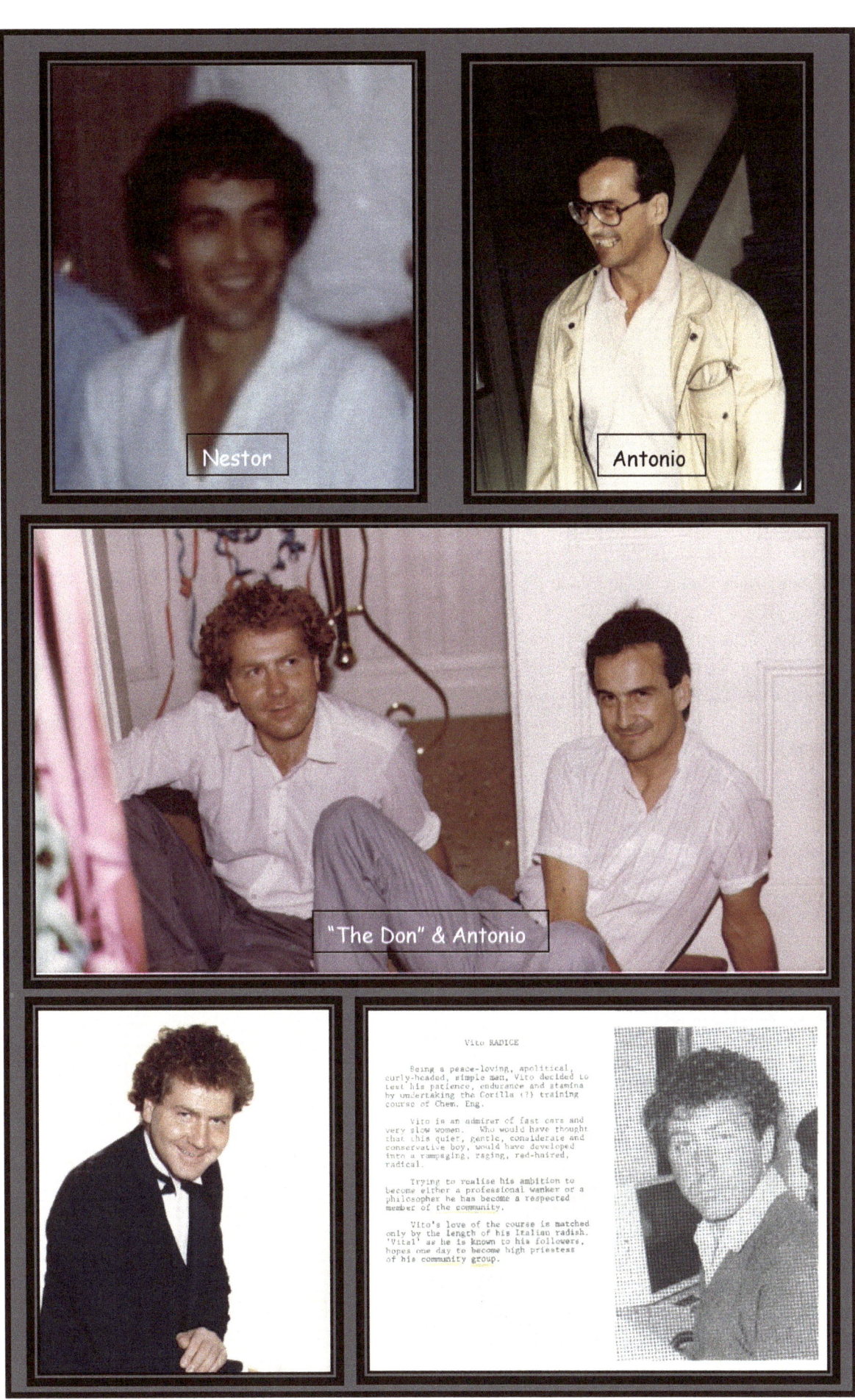

Chapter 17: The (Great) Escape *(from the nest)*
I gotta get outta of this place!

My father was an angry man!

On 31st August 1983, it was the afternoon and Greg was over. We were in the lounge room having a smoke (tobacco), having a glass of wine, Greg asked for some cheese and bread so I went into the kitchen where my father was sitting at the kitchen table fuming. I knew he was angry but I didn't know what he was angry about! Stupidly, I asked him and he just went ballistic. He blew his top, shouting at the top of his voice, pacing up and down the kitchen floor (he'd gotten up from his chair), frothing at the mouth, beating his hairy chest (he didn't have a shirt on, he was often bare-chested), going completely crazy!

The issue that had triggered this outrageous reaction was my taking cheese and bread to Greg!

How dare I do such a heinous act!

Offer cheese, bread & wine to my friend!

He didn't know him!

He didn't want to know him!

He was a stranger in his house!

He should leave!

"NEVER TRUST the PEOPLE!"

So that evening I decided to escape!

I rang Nestor and Angelika who were living in Summer Hill at the time and asked them if I could stay at their place! They had a spare room off the kitchen.
They said yes, so the next morning, I packed as much as I could into my trusty and very reliable, light blue Toyota Corolla, JOM403. It had a four cylinder 1.1 Litre engine (which, for you car enthusiasts will know, is a very small engine)!

What a car that was!

We had so many adventures with that car. It was truly an amazing vehicle. It never broke down, ran on the "smell of an oily rag". I used to put $5 of petrol every week. It was only supposed to carry four passengers, that's including the driver but I'm sure we managed to fit in eight once!
It was stolen and trashed on the 12th December 1989.
But I digress………..

I left that morning, the first day of Spring (1st September) 1983.

I was twenty-four years old!

I rang my mother that afternoon to tell her I had left. She had not yet been into my bedroom so she was still unaware. She started to cry and said "Come back, he's not home from work yet, he won't even know!" I told her I could not live there anymore! My time had come to leave and that I was sorry that I was hurting her but it was something that I had to do! She cried even more! So, I told her that I loved her and that would always love her, said goodbye and hung up the phone!

My brother and father found me in three days!

Apparently, I had left my little address book with my friends' names in it, so they rang them all asking if they knew where I was. Some of their replies to leaving were very funny, "Well, about time he left home!", "Congratulations!", "No, I didn't know but I'll tell him that you're looking for him, if I see him!", "Fantastic", "I'm sure he'd tell you if he wanted you to know where he was!", "He should've left a long time ago, if you ask me!" and "How old is he again?".

It was 1:00pm on the Sunday afternoon when there was a knock on the front door. Angelika went to see who it was. I was in my small room out the back. She came to call me and I could see that she looked very nervous, I asked what was wrong and she told me that there were two men at the front door, one of them said that he was my brother and that he wanted to talk to me.

I walked out through the kitchen, where Nestor was seated at the kitchen table, along the corridor which led to the lounge room in to the hallway corridor where I could see my brother standing outside the front door entrance, flanked by his father-in-law, Michaele. I walked past the two bedrooms and reached the front entrance and greeted my brother and Michaele.

All this time, as I was making my way to the front door, I was slightly nervous and anxious about what I was about to face and how to respond and handle it.

My brother told me that our father was in the Valiant and that he wanted to see me and talk to me. I walked out after them and followed them to where they had parked the car. My father was sitting in the backseat. I opened the front door and sat in the front seat. He was crying.

I asked him why was he crying? He said, *"Come home, I forgive you!"* I told him that there was nothing to forgive but I could not go home! He kept on crying and then he said *"Forgive me if I've done anything wrong"*. I told him that I forgave him. That I loved him but I could not go home with him. Still crying he said *"Even Jesus forgave those that wronged him"*. I repeated myself that I could no longer live with him and that it was time for me to leave. He said that I had a heart of stone. Upon which I said goodbye to him, opened the car door said goodbye to my brother and Michaele, who been standing a little distance away under the shade of a shop awning and went back to my new home.

My father was still crying.

I did not see or speak to him for the next six months!

In the *"Council Meeting of General Co-ordinators"* (the highest level in the organisation chaired by *Cobos*) of the 21st June 1983, it was decided that *"The Community"* would launch a political party to be called *"The Humanist Party"*.

The *"The Community"* would cease to exist!

This news was delivered to everyone by *Nestor*.

We were all SHOCKED!

A political party?

What did we know about politics?

The answer was a simple one: You learn by doing!

The reason: destructive events in the world were accelerating at a dangerous rate and that the only effective response to this time of great crisis was a political one.

We had to get our people in the political system and get our hands on the levers of power because those in power were destroying the planet!

How prophetic was that!

"The Humanist Party of Australia" was launched on Sunday 2nd August 1983 at the University of Technology (then, the Institute of Technology), Sydney.

The symbol of *"The Humanist Party"* was the **"Mobius Loop"**!

"The Mobius Loop", is an old geometric design (sometimes referred to as **"Sacred Geometry"**) which represents the interconnection between the inside of an entity and its outside.

They are but one and the same.

There is no distinction.

No separation.

No conflict.

No imbalance.

Perfect equilibrium.

Perfect balance.

Perfect harmony.

I was the President and spokesperson of the party (unanimously elected).

Chapter 18: The Humanist Party: Humanise the Earth

This was a scary proposition for me but I accepted the challenge with enthusiasm, good will and a lot of bravado.

It was a steep learning curve for me. I knew very little of politics so I had to learn fast.

And I did!

It was a new adventure for me and everyone involved and what an adventure it would become!

Straight away our weekly meetings became about political discussions and planning strategies and activities.

We had to make new materials, banners, leaflets, pamphlets, booklets, newsletters and newspapers.

Get involved in political activities and get members to join the new party.

To do this we went to the streets, stopped people, talked to them and asked them if they were interested and if they were, to join the *"Humanist Party"*!

"The Community" was DEAD!

"Internal work" was set aside!

Most of my friends who I had joined with and had introduced me to *"The Community"* left!

I was the last man standing!

It was a very steep learning curve. We had to write a constitution, policies, decide on political agenda, strategies and tactics. No easy task for political novices!

But we were committed and believed in what we were doing.

We managed to get *"The Humanist Party"* office in the old *Peggy Lee Building*, opposite Hyde Park, in front of Museum Station on Elizabeth Street, Sydney.

The rent was cheap and the location was to die for. Directly opposite Hyde Park on Elizabeth, just around the corner from Liverpool Street, Sydney!

The building was populated by all manner of people, arty, prostitutes, political parties, musicians, and other desperadoes and fringe dwellers!

What a *"multi-cultural"* community we were!

What a great location!

We had two rooms in this ramshackle of an old building. It even had one of those old style open-caged lifts.

It was truly a FANTASTIC place.

This was our centre of operations. One room (the larger one) on the third floor. was used for meetings and the second (smaller), was used for the production of materials, banners placards, newsletters, leaflets and as a general storage space.

- **The Campaign: Petition for a Referendum to Close Pine Gap (1985-198)**

The late 1980s were turbulent political times globally.
Ronald Reagan (former governor of California and b-grade movie actor was US president and Mikhail Gorbachev was president of the Soviet Union (USSR).

The biggest nuclear power plant accident in the history had occurred in Chernobyl, Ukraine in 1986 killing and injuring hundreds of thousands of people (an exact number has never been possible to determine), contaminating most of Europe and establishing a thirty kilometre radius exclusion zone for the next one thousand years.

The world was in a state of great upheaval and flux.

Nuclear disarmament was on top of the agenda for a lot of people and there were enormous rallies worldwide demanding action!

Australia was no different!

It was in this political environment that the lease for the US Military Defence installation in the centre of Australia was up for renewal.

The installation is called *"Pine Gap"*, a joint US-Australian run facility.
It gathers intelligence from around the world via satellites orbiting the planet, sending this information directly to The Pentagon.

This makes it an extremely sensitive facility and a first strike target, in the event of a nuclear confrontation.

Not a good situation for Australia to be in, I would have thought!
We took on the challenge!

We sought a referendum for people to decide whether the lease on "Pine Gap" should be renewed or not.

We thought that people should have a say on these vital decisions that directly affected their very existence!

Over a nine-month period from June 1985 to March 1986 we ran an intensive campaign collecting for a petition asking the government to have a referendum on this issue.
We campaigned almost every day, going out on the streets, talking to people and collecting signatures.

We went all over Sydney, put up banners, a card table with information and the petition for people to sign.

We also brought the "big gun", every protester's main tool of the trade, the *"megaphone"*!
This was quite daunting and scary at first. It takes a lot of guts to use one and it's NOT for everyone!

There are many ways to approach using a *"megaphone"* but it is not an easy instrument to use effectively!

There are those who shout into the mouthpiece, very emotional and expressing one's passion for their cause BUT not very effective because it is a very aggressive method. The message is physically distorted because the mouthpiece cannot cope with the barrage of vibrations and spit coming out of one's mouth, resulting in complete distortion, noise and abrasiveness for the poor passer-by. A very uncomfortable and sometimes painful experience. All a person walking past wants to do, is get as far away from there as quickly as possible.

Walk as fast as you can, don't make eye-contact!

A real TURNOFF!

Then there is the person who has a very high pitched, shrilly voice, again very painful for the poor passer-by.

Finally, there is the very softly spoken, almost whispering voice which is so unobtrusive, it negates the purpose of using the *"megaphone"* in the first place. One might as well be a statue. Completely ineffective.

My approach was to use a very modulated voice and allowing the *"megaphone"* to the work for me. I did not have the volume turned up to maximum, which instantly causes that annoying feedback distortion common to most *"megaphone"* users but is exactly the first thing most users do, in the mistaken belief that it is all about VOLUME! The need to be heard! On the contrary, the most important thing is to be UNDERSTOOD!
I used a low timbre voice, spoke slowly and clearly. I NEVER shouted!

People don't like being shouted at!

I tried to engage people rather than harangue them!

We managed to collect over 60,000 signatures!

An amazing accomplishment by such a small party!
We handed the petition to The Nuclear Disarmament Party Senator, Robert Woods who tabled it in Parliament.

Robert Woods was elected as a NSW senator in the 1987 Federal election. However, the High Court declared his election was invalid as he was not an Australian citizen at the time. He was not entitled to be nominated for election as a senator and therefore had never been validly elected. He was replaced by Irene Dunn, second on the ballot ticket.

It was our most successful campaign!

I was very proud of what we were able to achieve!

I still am!

- # The Elections (1984-1988)
  ### 1984: Federal Elections: NSW Senate
  Candidate: Vito Radice
  1st December, 1984

Our first real test was contesting the 1984 Federal Election.
The 1984 Australian federal election was held on 1st December 1984. The election was held eighteen months ahead of time, partly to bring the elections for the House of Representatives and Senate back into line following the double dissolution election of 1983.

We decided to field a candidate for the NSW lower house seat of *"Sydney"*!

Guess who the candidate was?

Yep! You guessed it!

Me!

This is what happens when you start something. You decide what to do!

Why?

Out of pure necessity!

There is no one else to do it if you don't!

I was twenty-five years old!

It gets much more complicated when more people are involved!

The *"Sydney"* electorate covered the inner city that included Newtown, Glebe, Marrickville and the city itself. It was a *"Labor Party"* held seat at the time. The sitting member was *"Peter Baldwin"*.

In hindsight this was probably a mistake. It would probably have been more effective and efficient if we'd contested the NSW Senate, because then electors from all over the state could have been able to vote for us, not just those living in the *"Sydney"* electorate.

A couple of things were against us from the very start:

- Small, unknown party
- Unknown candidate
- Limited funds and resources such as people to help
- Not about to use our logo on the ballot paper
- No media coverage

Not having the *HP* logo on the ballot paper was a huge disadvantage because people could not find us and I was a complete nobody!

To get the logo of a political party onto the ballot paper, the party is required to have a minimum of five hundred registered members or already be a sitting member of parliament.

Getting five hundred registered members, for a new party just starting out is not that easy.

It is no mean feat and quite an obstacle to jump over!

It is very, very difficult.

Especially, when people are apathetic and disillusioned with politicians and politics in general.

Nevertheless, we ran fearless campaign it was a fantastic experience for me.

Our campaign strategy was very simple: go out on the streets every day, stop and talk to people. At night we would go out and plaster walls with posters. My sexy, handsome face was everywhere. Especially in the Devonshire Street tunnel which we plastered both sides of the tunnel from end to end.

No one could miss me!

For glue, we would use the, every revolutionaries' tools of the trade: a bucket, a brush, flour and water.

The perfect glue!

Very cheap!

Sometimes we would use sticky tape, to put posters around telegraph poles but this was more expensive.

The incumbent *"Labor Party"* led by *Prime Minister Bob Hawke* defeated the opposition *"Liberal–National Party"* coalition, led *by Andrew Peacock*.

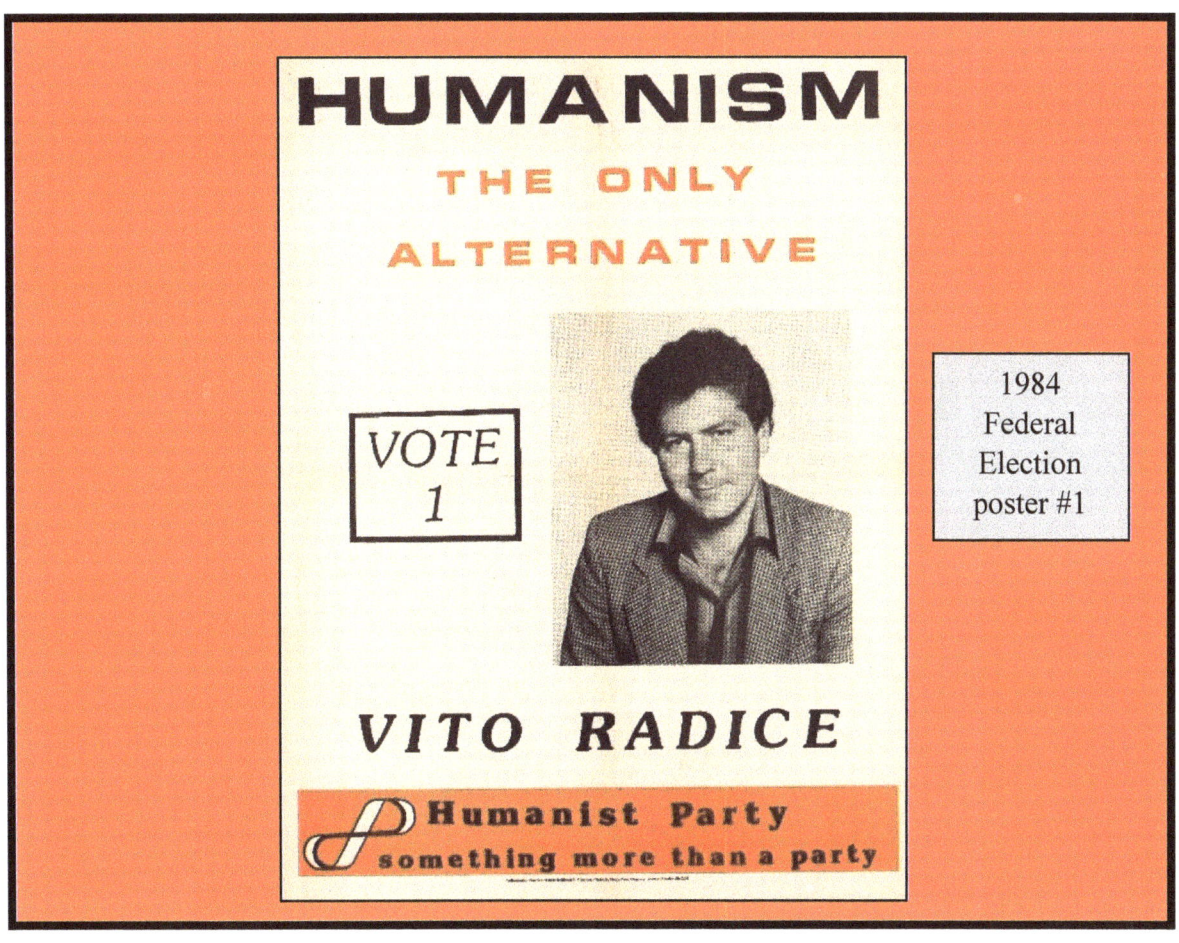

1984 Federal Election poster #2

- **Federal Elections: The Senate (19th March, 1987)**

- **Local Council Elections: Marrickville Council (26th September, 1987)**
  Candidates: Vito Radice, Scott Wilkie, Mariclaire Pringle

In 1987 we launched "The Urban Greens" because "The Greens" already existed here in Australia. This was in contrast to the already existing German *"Greens"*!

Antonio left Australia to resettle in the UK in February 1988.

Antonio soon after suggested that I travel to Europe and experience how the *"The Movement"* was operating in other countries. This was a great idea, so he organised an itinerary and for me to stay with other members.

So, in June 1988 I was off to England and Europe.

My trip started in London, Manchester, Glasgow, London, Paris, Milan and then back to London.

What a trip!

It was only for three weeks and it was truly and amazing experience!

The members that I stayed with were complete strangers but they were like we'd been friends for a lifetime beforehand!
We brought this new approach back to Sydney & implemented it straight away!

We had immediate positive results!
It was another fantastic experience and a lot of fun!

• The First International of The Humanist Party, Florence, Italy, 7th January, 1989

I also was fortunate enough to attend the *"First International of The Humanist Party"* held in Florence on the 7th January 1989.

Mariclaire and I left Sydney on an Air India flight bound for Rome, with short stopovers in Singapore and Mumbai (Bombay) on 3rd January, 1989. About five hours into the flight the plane started to descend, which I thought unusual. I was looking out the window as the plane was landing, I thought, "Singapore has changed, it's all rural!" We in fact had landed in Bali, Indonesia. It was an unscheduled stop. Once on the tarmac, we were told to leave the plane and go into the airport lounge. No one knew what was going on.

Once inside, all the Air India crew disappeared and there was no information given to us and no one to ask what was happening. Air India didn't have an office in Bali! It didn't fly to Bali!

Passengers were becoming frustrated at the lack of information and so some had communication with friends and relatives back in Australia. It was all over the news in Australia, "a threat had been received that an Air India flight bound for Singapore had a bomb on it!"

Us!

This was very scary as a plane had been blown up over Scotland and crashed in Lockerbie on the 21st December, 1988 only a few weeks earlier. Killing everyone on board!

It was a hoax! There was no bomb on board but it did disrupt our travel arrangements. We finally arrived in Florence via Hamburg on a Lufthansa flight from Mumbai on 5th January, 1989, forty-eight hours later!

The longest plane flight ever!

The next day, the 6th January, we decided to take a stroll and take in some of the sights of beautiful Florence. However, the city was blanketed in a thick layer of fog. You couldn't see a metre in front of you!

It was sublime!

The Duomo of Florence Cathedral emerged majestically out of the fog as if it was suspended in mid-air!
It was truly transcendental!

As we walked about, we noticed that there was no else about. The streets were all deserted! Where was everyone?

It was mid-morning, going on to lunchtime but not a soul was about?

What the fuck was going?

This was very weird?

All the shops and cafes were also closed!

By this time, we'd been walking for a couple of hours and we were getting peckish so we started looking for a place to have coffee and something to eat. Finally, we found a trottaria that was opened and went in. I asked them in my best Italian, *"Che cazzo sta succedendo oggi? Dove sono tutti? (What the fuck is going on today? Where is everyone?")*. He replied in quite an incredulous tone, *"Non sai cos'è oggi? Oggi, 6 gennaio, è l'Epifania! È un giorno festivo! È uno dei giorni più importanti del calendario cattolico! Tutti sono a casa a festeggiare! (Don't you know what today is? Today, 6th January, is The Epiphany! It's a public holiday! It's one of the most important days in the Catholic calendar! Everyone is at home celebrating!")*.

I felt like a fool!

I'd never heard of "The Epiphany" or the 6th of January as an important day and was a Roman Catholic! Supposedly! It was not celebrated in Australia!

I told him, *"Vengo dall'Australia! Non è celebrato lì! (I come from Australia! It's not celebrated there!")*. With this information he became very excited and told me all about *"l'Epifania (The Epiphany)"*

What a wonderful time!

Outside, the fog still enveloped the beautiful city of Florence but now we knew that we had it virtually all to ourselves.

What a magical experience!

As we were stolling about, in the thick mist/fog, we were approached by a couple, who stopped and asked us, *"Are you from Australia?"* I answered increduously, *"Yes! But how the fuck did you know that?"*. They answered, *"Who else would be strolling about a deserted Florence on the 6th of January?"*. They were right. The same thing had happened to them. They were also from Australia!
Spooky!
What a small world!

Another amazing thing happened was when we were travelling to Edinburgh, Scotland after Florence and we went past the Lockerbie crash site which was not far from the road. To my astonishment the cockpit of the plane was still there!

- # First International of The Green Party, Rio de Janeiro, Brazil, 7th August 1989

Cathie, Mariclaire and I were also able to attend *"First International of The Green Party"*, which was held in Rio de Janeiro, Brazil on the 7th August 1989.

- # International Joint Activity, Paris, August 1990

Cathie, Mariclaire, Linley and I also went to Paris and London for two weeks in July 1990, to participate in an international week long, joint activity in Paris.

We stayed with Stephane, a member, in his house in Vincennes which is 6.7km east, from the centre of Paris. His parents had gone on a holiday to Israel and so he had the house all to himself. Stephane could speak English very well and probably the reason he was asked to look after us. Which he did magnificently.

The house was a three-story, which in itself was fantastic but what really made extraordinary was that it also had a basement. The basement had a tunnel which connected to *"Vincennes Castle"*. Apparently, the tunnel was used for mistresses and lovers to enter the castle in secret. It was also supposed to be an escape route in case the castle was attacked.

We were organised into groups of about ten people and sent off to various locations throughout Paris to stop people on the street, introduce them to "The Movement", ask them if they were interested and if they were, take them directly to a space that had been hired and another person carried out an "Introductory Meeting", which at the end of, were asked if the wanted to join. This was all done with my almost non-existent French language skills.

The groups consisted of members from all different parts of the globe. It was truly a wonderful experience to interact, participate with all these different nationalities!

The idea was to accelerate the process of participation.

To reduce the time between initial contact & involvement & participation!

"Direct Communication".

A person could be on the street with us, stopping and talking to new people, repeating what they had just experienced, within half an hour!

Stop a person, ask them a couple of simple questions, take them to a locale or coffee shop or any other suitable location, carry out an "Introductory Meeting" which included a simple *"Experience"* (of *Internal Work*) and then ask them to join us on the street, straight away!
No mucking around!

It WORKED!
We brought this new approach back to Sydney & implemented it straight away!

We had immediate positive results!

It was another fantastic experience and a lot of fun!

Linley   Antonio   Cathie   Vito

Vito   Sherwin   Linley

It was late on a Monday night in February 1992. I had finished a weekly meeting at the Rozelle Neighbourhood Centre with Mariclaire and Cathy. We walked out onto Darling Street, Balmain and I said, "Guys I've had enough! I'm not going to do this anymore!"

And with that, I called it quits on *"The Movement"*!

The race was over.
I gave up!
I walked away from "The Movement", FOREVER!

Chapter 19: The Radice Code (RCF)

• Radice Code (School):

Its inspiration came from the movie *"The Da Vinci Code"* (I am not very original, as you can see. I just appropriate ideas and recontexualise them).

It was not meant to be a punishment system but rather a reward system for students. The idea was for students to take control for their own behaviours within the classroom.

It worked a treat!

It worked with every class and every year group, from juniors to seniors.

Everyone loved *"The Radice Code (RCF)"*!

The *"Radice Code-RCF(School)"* was based on 3 fundamental values:

1. **R** = **R**espect
2. **C** = **C**o-operation
3. **F** = **F**ocus

Steps in the administration of the **"Radice Code"**:

1. If a student broke any of these 3, they were given a warning and their names were written up in the **WARNINGS** list.
2. If they transgressed once again, they were given a 2nd warning and a x 2 was placed next to their names in the **WARNINGS** list.
3. If the transgressed a 3rd time their name now was placed under the **REPORT** list, meaning that if they continued to transgress, a report would be written and possibly sent to the Head Teacher for further disciplinary actions. The report stated: *"(Name of student) has been disrespectful, unco-operative & has refused to focus on the tasksset in class. He was given numerous chances to co-operate but has refused to do so."*
4. Redemption

I told the students that I believed in redemption, so a person who had broken the *"Radice Code"* could redeem themselves by following the *"Radice Code"*. So, this meant that students could redeem themselves and their names would be taken off the **REPORT** list or the **WARNING**S list.

If a student did not transgress the **Radice Code** throughout the whole lesson, I told the students that I would have 5 RCF cards to give away at the end of the lesson.

These cards soon became coveted and strongly sought out throughout the whole school!

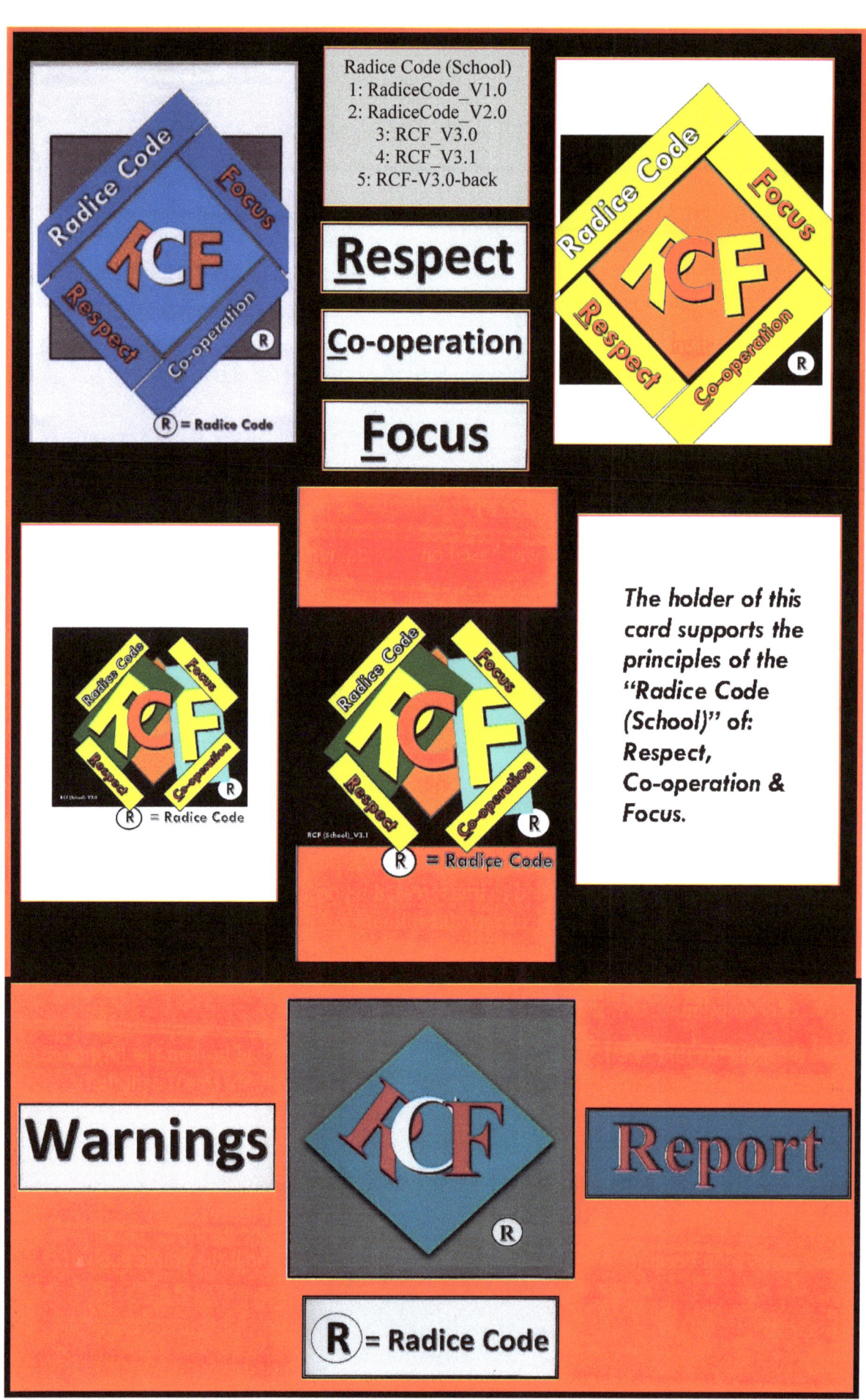

- Radice Code (Society):

This came from a suggestion by a student who said that he liked the **"Radice Code (School)"** so much, that there should be one for society.

So, the **"Radice Code (Society)"** was born.

The *"Radice Code-RCF(Society)"* was based on 3 fundamental values:

1. **R** = **R**espect
2. **C** = **C**ompassion
3. **F** = **F**riendship

This also proved to be very popular amongst students.

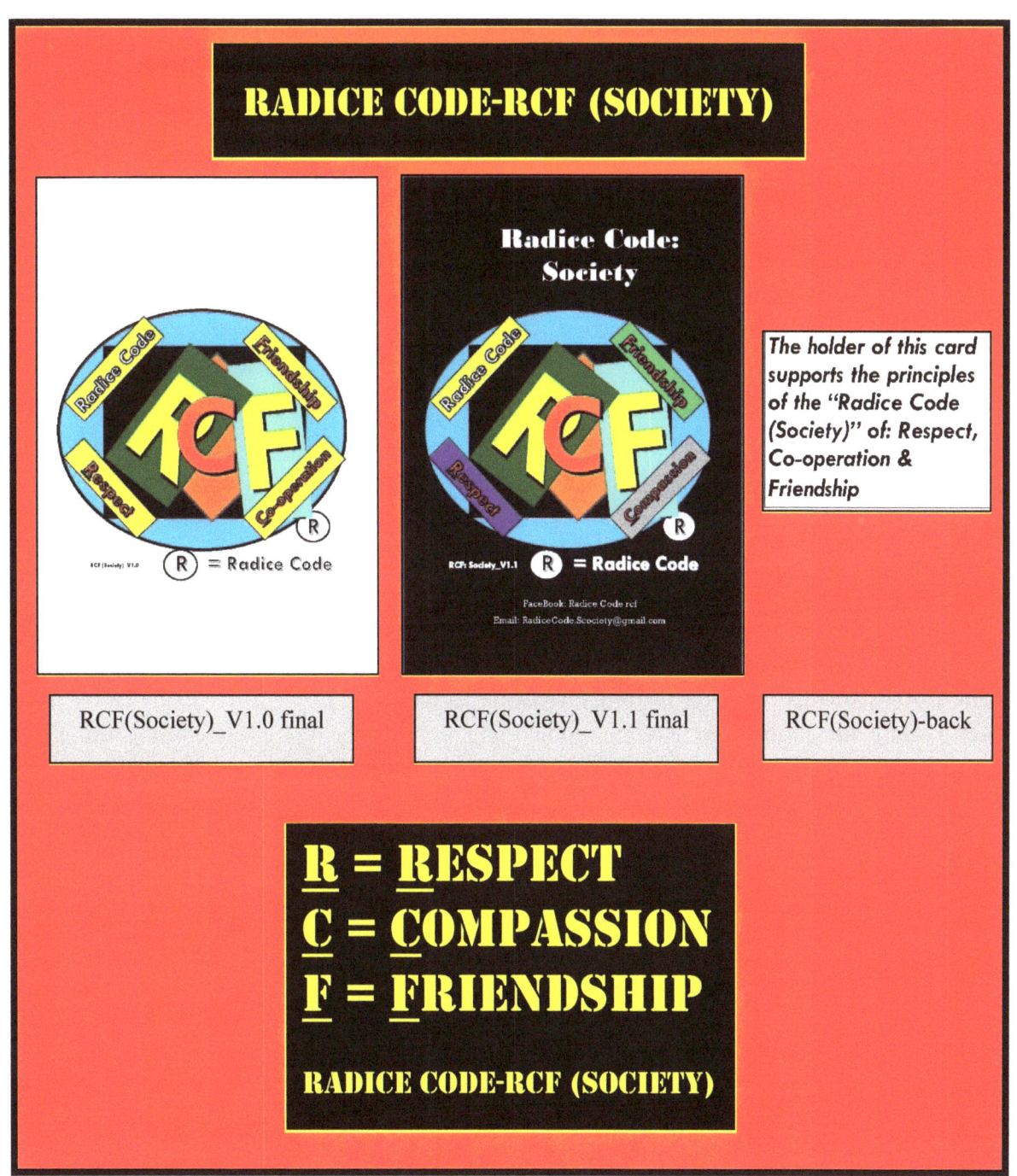

Chapter 20: Evolution of "The Don"

• The Polemicist (2016)

The Idea of "The Polemicist" came about by my friend Greg who one day said to me, *"Hey Don, you know what you are? You are a Polemicist!"*. He was absolutely right. I was a *"Polemicist"* and so from that moment on I adopted this idea of *"The Polemicist"*.

I was a *"Polemicist"*!

So, over the next few years I started to develop the persona of *"The Polemicist"*.

• "The Don" (2020)

"The Don" also came about from Greg. It was 1972 and the film *"The Godfather"* had just been released. It became an instant classic. It was about a Mafia boss whose name was *Don Vito Corleone*, *"The Don"* or in Italian. *"Il Padrino"*, *"The Godfather"*.

Greg started calling me *"Don"*, for obvious reasons and so, the name stuck.

From then on, I was *"The Don"*!

Since then, *"The Don"* has been my "Alta ego", my "Other persona". He is the performer, the extrovert, he has no limits, he has no boundaries. He does whatever the fuck he feels like, with whomever and wherever he likes. Why? Because he doesn't give a shit about anything.

"The Don" is FEARLESS!

He is WILD!

He is indestructible!

He is immortal!

"The Don" started performing, reading his poems, mainly at *"Sappho Bar"* in Glebe but also a few other places in the inner west of Sydney.

"The Don" has big plans!

I started writing poems on the 1st April 2020. I was texting my friend Brian & we were basically riffing backwards and forwards to each other.

Afterwards, I read it and I thought *"shit, this is good! I can do this. I think I'm a poet!"*.

This was in fact, my very first poem.

So, I started to write & I just couldn't stop. I date all my poems and so I know exactly what I was doing, thinking and feeling at that time. It's almost like a journal entry.

That's how it all started. Crazy but true!

I had found my purpose. I had found the meaning of my existence of this planet.

I had been searching my whole life, never knowing what I was here for & than, out of nowhere it hit me!

I am a poet!

And I've never been happier!

Everything fell into place.

I stopped searching.

I knew who I was!

I am a poet!

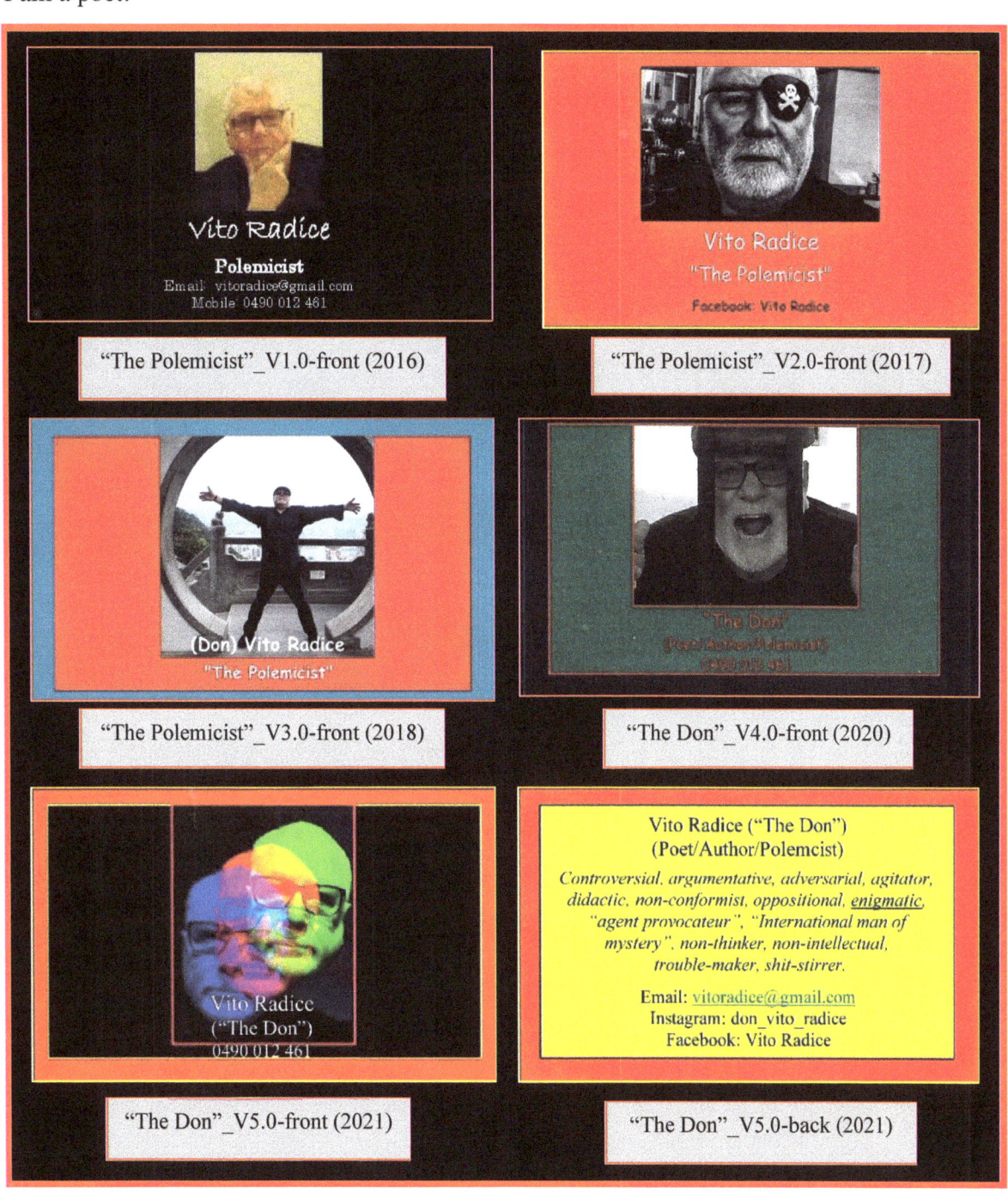

"The Don"
(2022)

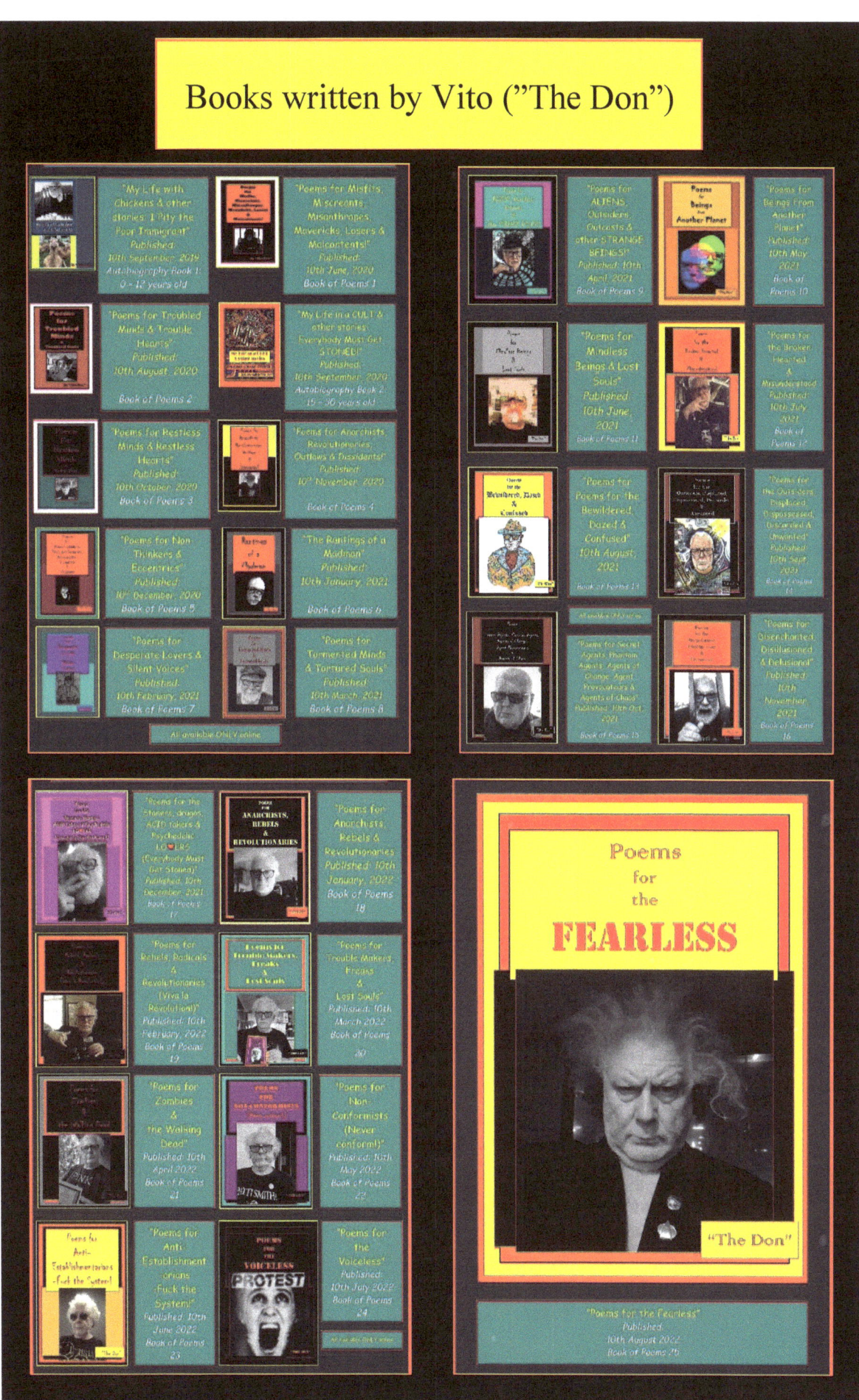

Chapter 21: Buona Vita-Be Creative

"Buona Vita-Be Creative" (2017) started out as an idea to start a social media webpage that I had control over rather than relying on *"Facebook"* or *"Instagram"* for me to get my ideas, thoughts and work out to people.

It then went on from there. I created and designed a website. I registered it as a company. It's aims to be a non-profit social media organisation, promoting, encouraging and inspiring creativity.

Buona Vita-Be Creative logos (207-2018)

Buona Vita (BV) is:

A concept, an idea, a MOVEMENT.

It has as its inception the need to make one's life better, fuller, with purpose & meaning.

BV promotes, encourages & supports people who want to make a difference, each in their own small way; whether it be through science, art, music, community activities & activities, craftspeople & the whole kaleidoscope of human activity.

BV provides a voice for these ordinary people to be heard, to be seen, a conduit for their expressions to be exposed to others.

BV is a network of the voiceless people that join together so that their voices will become a roar, load & clear.

BV: the voice of:

"Ordinary People Doing Extra-Ordinary Things"

Chapter 22: In the End……

My father died in the early hours of the 25th May 2008 at RPA Hospital in Camperdown, after a short illness. He was eighty-three years old. He had contracted *"septicaemia (sepsis)"* and it had spread throughout his body resulting in massive organ failure. There was nothing the doctors could do except pump him with antibiotics which prolonged his life for an extra three weeks. Watching him die in those last weeks, I learnt that it's better to come to terms with your demons put them to rest earlier in your life, when you can. Have the strength and courage to confront them, rather than wait and fight with them when you're dying.

My father was fighting his demons right till the end.

It was NOT a good death!

My mother is eighty-seven years young and is still living, by herself, in the family home in Elizabeth Street, Five Dock.

Make sure to have a good LIFE, so that you can have a good DEATH!

My father, Giuseppe Radice
(1924-2008)
Circa Nov' 2007

My mother, Angela (Martone) Radice
(1932-)
Photo taken by Mariclaire, 01.05.2022

The End

www.ingramcontent.com/pod-product-compliance
Lightning Source LLC
Chambersburg PA
CBHW061537010526
44107CB00067B/2898